THE NATIONAL POETRY SERIES

The National Poetry Series was established in 1978 to publish five collections of poetry annually through five participating publishers. The manuscripts are selected by five poets of national reputation. Publication is funded by the Copernicus Society of America, James A. Michener, Edward J. Piszek, the Lannan Foundation, and the Andrew W. Mellon Foundation.

1992 COMPETITION

Shorter Poems, by Gerald Burns.
Selected by Robert Creeley. Dalkey Archive Press.

My Alexandria, by Mark Doty.
Selected by Philip Levine. University of Illinois Press.

Lost Body, by Terry Ehret.
Selected by Carolyn Kizer. Copper Canyon Press.

Debt, by Mark Levine.
Selected by Jorie Graham. William Morrow & Co.

What We Don't Know About Each Other, by Lawrence Raab.
Selected by Stephen Dunn. Viking Penguin.

Shorter Poems

BOOKS BY GERALD BURNS

POETRY

A Book of Spells (1975)
Letters to Obscure Men (1979)
Boccherini's Minuet (1981)
Shorter Poems (1993)

PROSE

Toward a Phenomenology of Written Art (1979)
A Thing About Language (1989)

Shorter Poems

GERALD BURNS

Dalkey Archive Press

Some of these poems have appeared in the following publications: *American Poetry Review; Another Chicago Magazine; Best American Poetry 1991; Brief; Camellia; Dallas Arts Revue; Exquisite Corpse; Faber Book of Movie Verse; Fine Madness; Giants Play Well in the Drizzle . . .; Grand Street; Harvard Magazine; Hole; How the Net Is Gripped* (UK); *Ironwood; Lace Neck Review; lift; lower limit speech; Motel; New American Writing; The Perfect World* (catalogue, San Antonio Museum of Art); *Phone-a-Poem* (Boston): *Salt Lick; Scratch* (UK); *Screens and Tasted Parallels; Sulfur; Talisman; Temblor; We Are the Weird; Writing; 1990 Quarterly; 6ix.*

The differences in punctuation, possessives, capitals, italic and so on from poem to poem are the author's, and do not reflect the publisher's preference for standard usage. The author thanks the compositor for cleaving to his choices.

Library of Congress Cataloging-in-Publication Data
Burns, Gerald.
  [Poems. Selections]
  Shorter poems / Gerald Burns. — 1st ed.
  Includes index.
  I. Title.
PS3552.U73244A6   1993
811'.54—dc20   92-29476
ISBN: 1-56478-025-2 (cloth)
ISBN: 1-56478-026-0 (paper)

Partially funded by grants from The National Endowment for the Arts and The Illinois Arts Council.

Dalkey Archive Press
Fairchild Hall
Illinois State University
Normal, IL 61761

Photograph of the author by Clio Dunn.

Printed on permanent/durable acid-free paper and bound in the United States of America.

Contents

Shorter Poems

Silent Poems

Clarke on the Fo'c'sle; to Him, Burns

Any text is a manifesto, can make a poetics. A poem I just finished mentions a river god in
textile with fat urns the source of /a/ river, just blue and offwhite
thread, not even sad that it dulls down, even rolled in acid-free paper
and stored at constant temperature. Fetished iron and thread are a Nail God
for us, the hours you spent reading unwasted. Pope
cared like you for states of things but caressed them, surfaces as such, your fourteen-
liners so offhand shine here with that glow, odor of tea because
like Marianne Moore they pretend notes only are intended and this for courtesy
as much as scholarship. Primitive things should stay what they are.
"Power" in Blake isn't like what this company I set type for vends, physics and magic distinct.
As I read, argument pouring down the page Tennysonianly picturesque
you might I suppose construct this plasticine-limbed figure taken as talking *among* such
things or entities as Keats desiring fallen ones put himself on steps leading to them,
Vader or Conan images (again they can be called this because already made into
images), the message-poem like any lecture or sword grip
like brooches in *Arthur's Britain* plates, thing for David Jones to thumb, thinking
about rats, this trouble argument has of assuming an audience
moderately well disposed to *Sorge*fuls. It's gone, John, the Norns with magnetic fish,
William Morris off to Iceland (Gloucester). Gerrit says there's a Black Mountain
Bard event you may be at, everyone planting stone spindles and churingas
to be in journals, and don't you like (better than photos) ink renderings of flints, stippled.
I was in Gloucester Sunday painting boats, blue, black, blue, green, blue—they
had names but (like "Liberty" on a white one just a dot) not rendered, tiny
bit of scrollwork to stand for theirs, red speck for bicycle-reflector "eye" on by
good luck the green one, and calligraphy over kind of undulant (and
diverse) sky blue to be reflected masts, hung nets, mass of boats—the backs
notch in so so do the reflections—and it didn't matter that the wind shifted
when I was nearly done and the boats turned more toward me, gulls on the
roof painted in and painted out. Elizabeth Sewell (*The Structure of Poetry*) describes
Mallarmé as this network of nonreferential nouns (wrapped as everybody knows around
an absence) and there's just no reference there to reference of paint. My squiggles
are Monets seen in the Jeu de Paume of boats in rivers and what I was looking at equally.
And great single-figure calligraphs from karate-film *dojos*. Anything's a myth to me,
the kid's silver whistle-rattle in Boston's Museum with clusters of bells. Chinese bronze
harness bells, the rigid ones in a circle, could have inside, as clappers, small bronze bells
you can peer at, shadowed from verdigris and narrowness of aperture, like anything
in Currier & Ives. The world is almost intrinsically flotsam (if the box is big you live
in it, if small a bookshelf). Carved boat hulls and harpoons tinted on the living board
they're cut from say first this is decor, then ignore the board. The chips you see look
like brushstrokes. In the boat these people in Sou'westers remind
you (their job) of Ryder, Wyeth, complex of people who, spending themselves on
rendering gave us—Dracula in the Wild West—personage and context complete.
All this has been said before in Italian. Say I recognize your accent or
saxophone playing in the tomb, knock on the side (no carved figures to describe)
and you, rising, ask how Buffalo is. Neither you nor I is mythic but the saxophone
probably is. Verse is *for* this soapy rendering, "buttery" as Permalba white says
on the box, Apollo's robe in the tapestry like a Vermeer wall map.
Johnson's *Lives of the Poets* in the Chandos reprint (spotted in Abraxas) once you
get past the foreedge marbling and spidery title page are a manifesto (what do you
think of "manifestion"?) for a kind of art, or is it any at all
you're afraid will go, Pope under squamous poetastrian deformers . . . potty silver

creamers of the period can have, instead of gryphon feet, trim hooves, the effect
startling as (really seen) those bells with bells inside, the balls inside *those* stone.
I go eighteenth-century, think of Gosse's *Gray* in the same shop, "Elegy Wrote in a
Country Church-Yard" for the tastes of scholars for whom study is a flavor.
To be a "thing" at all, Kant says, a thing has to be one of a series. There are no
unique events. Any poem contains a poetics as (Aristotle) a resonant event its maxim.
A bottlecap is a shield (a young man I talked to said you can flatten them and make
a snake.) Film projected through smoky lucite is demiurges, -urgos, and Apollo's name
ends with n.
Regularity can be specified, Black Mountain Alums Convene at Bard. *Omphalos* is
a long oval puddingstone rock from Don Quatrale's yard he stuck upright in a pot.
Everything, absolutely everything is a herm and hence a poetics, if a poetics is what
helps you think about something. The stories as you say, in their localia, recede even
for peasant retailers, word in French. If the elephant blanket is embroidered
with jewels, it doesn't matter at all that the elephant is silver. I'm leafing through
Thomas's *Collected Poems,* dark-vowelled birds, heads in a cunning cloud,
the last lines, "as long as forever is," fern's seeds on the sill, girl-encircled island . . .
saint heron on kingfisher shore. We wear their sounds like plaid pins (found in graves
till the Christians stopped burying them). Scotland had mirrors, and *images*
of mirrors carved on rock, vestige if you like vestiges of an old religion, and we're
told by Ricks the Lady of Shalott used her mirror to see the good side
of her tapestry. This too is poetics, art meditating on the *fact* of image as established
by craft. Ashbery curved what curved before. Escher's spheroidal maunderings reflect
nothing, his lizards gollies. You before the mast (I suppose that big thing is a mast)
as Hart sinks bubbling behind and Olson's Figure of Outward does so, cut tin,
do wangle in with feathers so hard to make of iron (I've worked for people
who gilded leaves) and the duck we kept in the bathroom left tufts of down we still find
and the gold leaves in Franklin's static tester *could* be iron. You could amalgamate
a blue feather under glass in an iron brooch to wear with a plaid, down Derry down.
Inside the shadow under the lip of the Chinese bell you see, dim as a strict interior, this
sphere pierced with a grin as it were, slot for sound, through which the pebble that's its
    clapper cleeks.

Looking into Dryden's Virgil

Now out of favor perhaps for having written quite so much
Dryden standing like a gentleman, one knee a little bent
the ships below like windup pavement toys or vehicles
plying arterial on airlanes in sepia *Metropolis* define
by ignoring us the insouciance of the patroned
or movie for which you need not entirely vote, Leiningen's "Madam"
leaving an edge free neither belief nor action
(the stole unnoticed over the confessing priest's shoulders).
We go from long E fields-sheep-trees-bees to Junoesque
S: Thus rag'd the goddess; the restless regions of the storms she sought
whom? Aeolus whose vacuumbags imprison "spacious" and "sounding"
as one might wear green latex gloves while pruning plants
—the fat green book on botanical Latin seen yesterday that. Swell
in undersyntax is deduced from smooth (of waves), all
Expell'd, exil'd, banish'd, transfix'd, oppress'd, vanquish'd

as Aeneas, suppressing his Primal E in a diphthong, collaborates with her.
Latium the white milk into carved bowls won in contests and Corydon pronounced like
    corridor
subsist below waves, sea, raging billows, bring streams that Triton and
nymphs green as nymphs restrain by a shift of adjective.
Heartened by hodgepodge, Delacroix's sirens biting each other's scalps, we see
Wordsworth dressed as Triton, bobbing up and down (an
embarrassment like a nautilus shell pendant too heavy to wear
yet desirable; Some dry their corn, infected with the brine.)
Diction may be what distinguishes us from him but the long-a
sustain-restrain, wait-gate, remains-chains, a dozen as if infected by "Faith" above
bound like poor captives on a column neck to neck or triplets'
bracket. Our neighbors build a wood fence to screen our dumpster
(maybe, they don't say) all we can do is photograph or sue.
This country of the mind in which Homer and Virgil connect
demands the flattening of a syllabus no longer common
as under a cover slip two drops of water mingle.
Each character, pretending to inform, talks of what's known
the stamp you send like the one you get on the envelope I send you,
over and over Ceres' ploy, they skim the ground, and seek the quiet stream.
Builds theaters, paints on the wall "See there, where,"
vessels more valuable than their gold (massy plate) likewise illustrated—
the heft, everything marble like an MIT paperweight, beneath, the verse rotund.
Laocoon and his children et by serpents, his umlaut invaded by "winding volumes"
only religious as is the space invaded by links—
we say "plain speech" of this but it isn't; Greek braziers burn Roman charcoal
as Ficino, mad for Greek, would throw fennel on and sing
and Matthew Arnold want it luminous and unhokey, Celtic dream
of piety absorbed in the stylized bear on your pommel. "Their images
they hug," say of a flag made from captured flags, the conjurer's
restored handkerchiefs with each other's centers
if, at this point handed to the lenders, that were it
invisible stitching, lost like Creusa, pale specter to strike dumb the hair
that bleeds when pulled and says "I'm Polydore." Dante's fizzes.
"Dryden" looking more and more like Aeneas, lambda for diphthong
this nothing is, Lamb's dreaming of Celaeno, harpy.
If trees were forests they would "show their weapons" (Barbara Jordan);
these lay down theirs, soaking everything in ferric solutes
color nearly of this library discard's buckram.
Skip the results of a posture neither reading nor study
though his English breaks into letters like street signs in Irish
the uncial with its accents a pretty word for garbage
diction one's response to piecing out bruscar
as Triton's car, no imposition, has for driver Wordsworth
august enough to calm the waves though it wasn't his taste to
(leaving, as we leave the club bore, Dryden by this means)
his plastic tendrils like a lagoon creature's iconic, enchanting.
There is no public voice is a sign for a building, Longfellow Place
here that which has across the street a yellow house
with a garden and little stones right out of the Romaunt.

Poem with Holes In

Whitman thought his ruddiness meant health, whereas we know
it merely meant he was more likely subject to a stroke, numbers
of which took him down though he still took air baths
nude and probably hankering. Spaces, as one's body is, must be insert
ed in the world, no preposition /in-to/ appropriate to
this graininess (Frost's "To Earthward," Creeley all objects being dirt) come
giddy as grit   to it   carborundum or mock-diamond mating
and Whitman, who left room even for BLANK SPACE . . . Bo Brown and his brother
would decide on a window in the cabin they're building and cut it out with a chain saw, no
OBJECT (or swan) so fine   you can set space but can you write space

An art book says Manet's model's book (or books) in the "Railway Station" may not
be a railway guide but verse
               you look a second differently at the blowup's
               horizontal smears   is that print?
the proof that it's on the page irregular. A detective story
by H. C. Bailey demonstrates an early manuscript is forged
because the text goes *through* a sheep's eyehole   vellum
It wasn't a lacuna but became one, a silence like Marianne Moore's choosing not to say
        something
that translates as a request to be taken out for veal or orangeade.
Rat   mirror   rat: imagine a virtual word
in a book by Lewis Carroll, mouse tale's curl to diamond type
and the eye listens rather than reads toward the end

Why isn't it all wonderful? the world's margins have margins
Elmslie's buttocks under gauze painted on his robe, Whitman prankster under the mask of
        Maugham, *The*
                    Summing Up
a space (you'd want to argue) parasitic on what props it
Samson's palms moist on pillars rough from lack of technique
                       or
            finegrained marble   copper chisel
Consider his spent body saying all the time I am softer than rock
ancestral observation that any hill could be or have been a grave
                any two hills
and the conjurer's cups, traditionally three, may really be holes
fists of air fixed by fiat, vertical as Louis XIV's long coat, the frills of it pretending to be
subject to gravity.
Better a squat dynamo, as in the back rooms of the MIT Museum generators donated by
        Edison
have sticking out (in odd places that look rotational) vacuum tubes
now patently what they were by imagining a *fluid* not thinkable as what drives the
                  microchip
                 tie   tack
sold there. It's not true we know what we know. We only know about it.
Suffering gives us genuine holes. McAndrew's deeferential valve-thingy, plans burned
as a monk might tear up drawings from a gospel quill—we imagine
mice near archaeologically displayed food and so there were, in London
               stuffed ones by a plate of oysters on a floor   Roman tile
the spaces for lost objects and predated food, as Pound'd say

of the process

a Samson of taste transcending taste   his cage and case now taken up
hole in our history . . . Whitman, visited, talked. Life's this walking *around,*
may be, motility or Pound's imagining that shores are to be traced, stood *out* for, what's
it mean a thing's in your arms, "have" you what you have, do you
(she asked, asking) like   it
Stein who did also ("beside," she'd say and leave the comma out)
wonder or at least ask if you mention a goat rope and tree in that order are they in that, in what
space, as I said to Clio   as: left   so: right
Moses's brother's breastplate jeweled like a book, smoky and rough
                                  smaragdinate
as a curled and perfumed beard or the shiver in your unwashed Crowley cuffs
who scared the people of Café Royale by drawing designs they scribbled under a dancing
     pencil end
in spite of which there's no power in directions as such, the text hole a consequence of
                    print
                    brush
                    forgetfulness
                    oxidant
                    habit
or wishing a line to begin anywhere, lunch with the New
gie't us, candlesticks in the shape of kissing people, written doily,
interstitiality   reticulated network   art

Fuzz and Porcelain

Tennisballs dyed green suspended with red ribbon in the sport shop
good in their way as Williams's white plastic deer dwarfed by greens
he wrote a poem about after do not, unaided, evoke a season. Their codes
drag on to the stage heraldic as a wyvern on Wedgewood, plastered
as the word Spode. Judith holds Holofernes, dripping, on sixteenth-century
Florentine ware, the verb for once not suspect; a knight
sleeps (more an inference) on an inkstand, on another a dragon *has subsided* to
     decoration.
The plates are round, the stands have pots for ink and plumy quills,
panniers on a level. Notre Dame, the towers hollow, could be this. You don't
reduce the figured thing, quite, green tennisballs not like limes.
Say rather the House of Usher, glazed on a plateful of ink like the
pitchers made of authors' heads, Dickens, Poe . . . anyone
recognizable may be *made* to pour.
That Taung skull with separable jaw (so decorative as *National Geographic* hologram)
appeals to me partly from having been so crushed as barely saved
then in its narrowness, held in the hand like a "boat" for incense,
almost a slipper shape and of course compassably small. No verb applies
to what it does unless it can be said to present itself
like a disease.
I saw (reprise) them again on the way to Auden's *Longer Poems,* each globe
"there," weakest verb, on wires, visually inert, each with a bow.
The extant, brute by mere, clobbers us, some inflammation of ball swollen by holiday
a condition even conditional as "this can become this," Wenceslasians caroling.
Byron, thou shouldst, Auden, tooth crack'd on a baked thimble, thou . . .

addressing the dead *is* to front these fuzzy balls as heads, forestalling song.
Even a mirror image, static as Ayer's Rock on this month's *Rotarian* cover
described seems vigorous, fusée as Cremorne Gardens you scan for sparks
Gulliver treating the plowed fields as corduroy.

In her Selected Poems

All those nice New England poets, each with a biography
we now find secondhand, remaindered (Haffenden's two dollars only)
it's as if the country bleaked at once, wild coast, into these white stones
or the palest moonstones Coursey mounts over tiny craters carved in silver
in rings. Ah, Riverside imprint! The area seems to wear its poets.
We dangle from earlobe, trail off the little finger like something in Beardsley, emperor or
    Georgian
fop. These were people who could use the word rhinestone in a poem.
They'd paid for it. A student I had who then went mad may have learned from them
verge utterance reckless as any similitude from seeing the faith in it
disjunct as a sacrifice, knife blade into goat's throat, the awful vowels
stained by adjacent consonants, whales in a black and white foyer.
I don't regret she's dead, or wrote so much it has to be condensed
liking the risk of choosing balance in Wakoski's to Sylvia, *Greed 9*
faces like strange moons, Vermeers, pearls on the museum wall's forehead
or creature masticating cardboard boxes you borrow from the supermarket to move
—this is no history of your peculiar amalgam of obloquy and fame
and Butor is right, on Cordova, that some relations demand the you
as Newton, once, the Muse, or Freud, your chains what Shelley's artisan makes
as you say, nothing personal. A Dallas winebar restaurant's anniversary rings were silver
grapes and leaves and a marvelous purple stone, also cabochon
taking in tone that highbreasted gown Josephine thought looked kind of Roman.
You are, even semiprecious, apparel. Egyptian plaster heads in tombs
always so deliberately unfinished we thought must be wig blocks, sideburns
or cap marks hacked in and always found overturned, on floor litter
left by the thieves as without value tell how to be, dreaming, the theories would say
(in this extended comparison right out of the workshop), ultimately
unwearable, not attire at all, or like the model cots with strapping
Ulysses and Rameses went to bed on, not originals at all but still not to be touched
greenstone cats with gold earrings, pretending like them to be aristocratic.
You still wrote too much, but your grace is no poem with an ending suits you.

Dan Sestina in Prison

In view of mouthfuls being neither air (think of them in a vacuum) nor chains
as if one were condemned to buying bread in Provençal, the
thudding tz's more like Metz than Arezzo, send us instead
lightness as of pastel flowers (or the violets on this sheet, growing from heartshaped
    leaves), a

shovelful of meaning, "turf" as that on which you bet never turves, impossible plural.
    Study me, imitate
yearning in tongues defunct. There is a pleasure to Henry James on Italian ruins with their
    reproductions in color
warm as tombs overgrown in a last Fragonard, ragazze waving at each other, laughing, the
    wash
taking air negligent as passports. We (classical) end a poem on strong sense,
not inconsequence.
A letter found in a book (preferably airmail-thin blue) is always in a
foreign language, talking about sixties presidential elections, or Canada, as the
first sight of a policeman dressed differently is travel. Pound
perambulates Provence, lunch in a sack, the words required to get lunch also bagged
—Berryman on airplanes locking in words with a broad nib. Whitman opens a milkweed pod
to touch silk seen. It's all emotionally speaking part of one's imagining of Italy
the naked Neapolitan fisherboy's cap, like a magician's bag in which an egg is hid, red
as in the Bert Lahr sketch the dancer's skirt conchitaed up, his
Roman truncheon.

For J. R. Here

To make the protospine a hollow sphere of cells invaginates, creases
inward like a zipper or the little tube some can make the tongue into (that's genetic—the
    best blow
bubbles made of spit). Compton and I took the A elevator up Crow's notched building
to where the slot . . . invaginates, high up, too much white marble but a view,
of Crystal Palace envying Crescent lacery, opera house in progress like a turtle,
one building an obsidian grand piano, I not liking to look down look up
to this quite narrow aperture not anything rigid's wingspan, abandon thridding.
I've been gone three years. Woke up in Tolbert's workroom to loveliest seascapes
looser black lines under, painted over, painted out. To Walker's where he shot me
wrapped in sculpture and by proxy quarters Bronco Bowl, Baudelaire and Verlaine
one frame per coin. (Trammell calls about our Institute reading for which the ad's my
    starnosed mole.) These
long lines are long life to us, go back to Kenneth Irby's "A Set" I saw first in
a flyer from Lawrence, KS where Burroughs chats with Cage whose spitbubbles
may remind us with Zukofsky the heart of the bluebonnet's black. Anyone can learn from
    anything,
biology, a building columnar as thighs wet from a pool, Darth Vader's mouth a groin
French as a park, separate as the stripe around a Galloway cow (together both colors of
    Guinness)
that makes it look while grazing hoist in a cargo sling's what being back feels like to me.

Things Like Names

Hermia (in Zukofsky's Stratford) was short, yet knowing his fancy unchunky as a herm
    that marking
the limits of a field was no Egyptian convention but that at base of which flowers
to the beyonders could be set, a crust, so like a grave marker but no paperweight for ashes,
    orphan lithos (accidentally
singular), more a shellcase humidor it'd be pointless to have two of.
To think a Stratford inhabitant like a character is odd, fingering too quickly
the pigskin Indiapaper plays as if impatient to *get to,* anyone accusable of it. Fetch
a comparison, they used to say, Shakespeare dwelling on it when Autolycus is driven
to name flowers, not technical like Stevens's (azaleas and so on), but country names
lived into, as somehow these on little cards in with the glass flowers (so odd
next to their translucent organs, laid flat in their fragility like something peeled from
    Ophelia's dress)
infected by their simulacra tilt as "Dickens," "Newman," "Gladstone" don't in
    Tussaud's, labels
for ideas of these, but a long palm frond or something with long spiky leaves like
tarragon, bland small versions of tobacco cultivated even in Connecticut
call the names in question, act of classifying. Elsewhere in Peabody
groundnesting birds or their nests in square boxes, grasses sticking up look vendible
as in a Scarborough Fair everything has a dragon on it and people address you in funny
    speech.
Curiosity that never quite fades into study shown the glass flowers at Harvard as a wonder
accepts these, hysterically beautiful Copan heads (so hard to give names to, to be English
    about)
and in a nearby case what seem hundreds of worthless fired-clay heads, the
trashiest trash till one, paler than the rest, stylish Mexican hair in wads
breasts trendy and a mouth, ah more herself in her opacity than
roosters whittled out of tourmaline.

Saint Femina's Liquefaction

Clio found Harlen's iron on end identical to Fatima in plastic
(her gold crown revolves for us) how wellspoken we can be about
Rose of Lima prototype of roseleaf or transomed boat, Beardsley our
spiritual advisor more useful than Munch's Sick Girl for retracting
his highheeled courtiers all Antoinette with ribbon'd crook, entrance refined
to aftertaste. Rose anyway, the celebrated pneumatic rose, inflatable gown
(where have we seen that) like any holy painting on tin with the tack holes
are only remarks about the allure of the feminine subverted (by gender
or vocation, these twain, simple variant on the lipsticked nun) go up
by sheer insistence of style, thriftshop shoulders emblematic now of menses, *blut* the
male poets pretend they want—to *write* in, Gansz's reviewer says. Fill the boiler with it
like St. Januarius's turning liquid on the day to ooos, otherwise crusting to a woody solid.
It's nothing for a man to wear a stock, bows on pumps. No one thinks he oozes
rests on a discharge, sharpening toward the top. Why envy what the teen finds onerous,
and Lucy (all bones, Witch of her own Coös) or the Taung one, brain endocast, likely
    female

might grin at flints smeared with "smear" discharged at one. Higgins colored inks mixed
   coagulate,
pull up sticky thready on a brush, umbilical to the parent puddle.

Boston Weather

"At one o'clock this morning humility is one hundred percent" and a
good thing too, kind subway drivers asking again where you want to go, no Somerville
drivers butting into traffic, no one stopping for accidents. There is
still error but no vice, since Aristotle says any virtue's prior
to the rest, magnanimity his choice, the armor with gods on, hunting scenes.
Foxes play in the streets, Gray's "Elegy" the merest reporting
that what is, is. In the subway Harpo Marx meets Edgar Poe waiting
for a train. Neither speaks. His brow so wide and luminous, those troubled eyes
look into his bugged-out ones. They advance, Harpo's knee somehow in
the other's hand, bobbing slightly as if on a spring. Cardinals
spray-paint their robes. I remember Cushing's fire engine pumps with
gold buckles followed by an acolyte in a fall of white lace and
magenta chasuble, his long cape (like the flag) not touching
anything, voice that learned to pray speaking political things on the backs
of trucks to hods. Give us, clotty weatherman, the prudence
of your description, what to wear, our cape miraculous
as chastity, rain pattering on the corrugated iron of our minds, no
error unhandleable, today, our starched breastpocket handkerchiefs
become bandana.

Boys' Bottoms and Swimming Pools

is the remark, so much easier to make than dyed paper scraps moulded in
memory of impasto, paint as a history of width, pasthe, thickness
that you want so a clarity you know will satisfy, floor squid
tap dolphin, thing detachably connected to water.
Now at this silly Ferry concert, smoke high by the flies as if barbecue, spots
purest lilac, foot speakers everywhere like mortars
—forgive me, I've not been to one of these, uneasy as at
a reference leaving me unsure how much of its familiarity to admit.
Mighty pleasant, sir, in his little white socks.
Syrian overtones everywhere. It could be Rome.
Interesting. They've now achieved a taupe bounce lighting.
Bright adjacent dyes mime diffusion of attention perforce
through a medium only partly transitive.
Sing in a pink spot, shadow like Mickey Mouse in a cartoon finale.
Wash isn't the word. I still don't see how they change their gels.
The whole effect is probably identical to looking at a boy's bottom through water.
Well, he makes more than Igor tootling his way through "Chinese Food" on a tenor sax.
It's been a heat wave. We've been worried about money. Clio oscillates beside me.

This revolutionary figure looking like lead dressed like Gainsborough (town of Mansfield,
    WWI)
did not improve close up, puttees invisible
in light from Shell.

Lines Broken Off

And here (the day after it) a flyer for Butterick's memorial service, same mail as a poem
by P. O'Reilly of the Boston Police for Detective Griffiths, the
beat of his three-line stanzas an approximate English hexameter, "in the
battle for truth, justice" George's, the card proposing a reading from Ruskin.
When Duncan died Michael Franco assembled many in Tapas's basement, Californians,
Bard people, even Ferrini, and read one beginning as so many of his do in the kitchen, halls
between rooms settling into the light there before going into his dream of finding the wake
in California in a highschool basement, details embarrassing as Duncan's details could
    make uneasy
his verse's uffings shoots from the avocado nut trailing and hairy, what good
even to writers of elegies ease to be naming the person, permission accorded solitary
    companions.
He showed me the Olson papers in Babbidge and either showed or described so vividly the
    watersoaked bales
of others that went through fire ("impossible to separate") it's as if I've seen them, rows of
    unreadable nauticalia and *little magazines* so
much the blood of him, then dinner with Ralph Maud at the Vernon Stiles where Richard
Potter, first important American conjurer may have performed and it was quite like seeing
    Johnson with Wilkes
to see the Olson scholars together at table, commensal, the intelligence of it how study
    especially
leads with its chin, saltshaker of quarrels resolved or irreconcilable allowed to be serious still
not flattened like tarsoaked cheesecloth smeared with more tar on a roof, passion part of
what is endured by scholars and poets, cannister shapes of Longfellow Bridge's towers
leading into Boston, gilt dome an impossible egg in morning light there.

Autumn Garden

MidOctober and all come into the sere, "Dear city of Cecrops," MacNeice's way of
making our town mayor wrap himself in mothy spots, the Luna nearly an eye
for that we're a municipality, across the street clipped shrubs, hedges something to feel
with the fingers on narrow walks for the old nuns to come (at right angles to) the
Virgin back-curved as Balzac not two thirds human height in front of Bocklin evergreens
in an attitude of prayer as if carved out of salt, the walks sweepable, hedge trimmed square
reddening in cold. It makes sense to come there in what might be real estate
garden really a vacant lot, more so in coolest citron Connecticut light. Our Congregational
church endeth in a square Norman tower, nail through wire igniting roof
above the clock all fire through cracks, the steeple finial perked sideways for
escaping smoke just like a teakettle but frightening, frightening while, other end
of the Common, her back to it Our Lady, suave as Eric Newton would say in her back curve

is about other errands thinking she is prayed to, at. The church's windows farther from the
 street have colored glass.
Its clock first stopped at 8:58 got moved by water to 11:30, limp as the hands on a dead Christ.
We hear ten shots, four four and two, as if the Poland Street massacre in Hillman's
 driveway, still
occupied by horse trailers and things. Why is the statue outdoors? because there things can
 happen to it,
as my indoor film shows so blue, icicles on their petite sign as the word "verger"
calls up a black patch about to move off its space.
Nature revels in a disinclination to fixity, swirling like Chagall's memory
around this lump put in the garden to prevent it boiling.

Believing Verse

So that's the point of it, Keble as Ella Wheeler Wilcox, lyre with angel heads
imagined as singing already so why not, around where the waist'd be emeralds squarecut,
 horizontally
in a line, around each diamonds and under nothing. Yet he was sure of his sexuality
in relation to his poetry, not unrelated to the surety with which (bubbles from the angelic
 heads'
lips if you imagine them as divers) he versified, the notion of verse as tune,
song in the drawingroom a thing rehearsed, ti tum. Grasp belief as on a Greek vase one
 grasped the wrestling
opponent's genitals, easy for us (Hughes and all) to find some flick of fire in the glass eye
of a stoat vivid in its hemisphere as pens turned rightside up denude their mannikins
or window in Nat. Hist., you push a button and paired ermine, engulfed in snow, whiten.
The waistcoast swells, voice booms, the panto view's dissolve restores the ruin'd tracery,
 within
falling like headless Victoria this apsidic voice, of Newman floated precisely as if triangulated
above a clover carved repeatedly in oak, in stone, lys manqué
always the notion of a voice issuing from something absolutely still
like a digital clock, or how Olson described Shakespeare's late verse powered by nothing.
It's character, how the candle takes the corner of the eye
that stays, heartstoppingly, circle of admiration left around what's irrevocably gone, the
inference from gray sink ring to white white hands, Sitwell's,
Keble's, Wilcox's, Newman's cast in bronze at either ends of rows of books.
The sphinx is patently mute, the beetle does not sing but fiddles, one amphorashaped
charcoal bluegray with orangeish bright-pink patterns on keeps toward the ground on bark
 of trees.
They said they sang but laid their eggs on that which they knew lived, or had lived
and this is never wholly fair as The Holy Family elides the word family and praying hands
don't even allude to Dürer's but to praying hands, such confusion of what one takes for
 granted.
Nude masses in a hedonic line applauding the setting sun turn in that moment
from terracotta dusted with gold to bluish browns, hands likewise for a moment paired
behind French blue clouds opposite another, higher, pink, the effect not necessarily
 Italianate.

Gratuitous Speech

The woman, perky as a parakeet, who talks in the subway to no one at all, no one at all
has a knit gray sweater today, talks of straitjackets, politicians, her sister, the
hair grayish white, pearls in or at least clipped on her ears, has us for audience
whether we want to or not. Everybody knows what she sings, not Wordsworth's solitary but
this is how Boston solitaries, mostly snappish, cranky do prattle on anywhere, in the street.
   She
times her silences, quiets when the train's becalmed, at best mutters, maintaining eye
    contact
not with us but with the audience we would be if we were. At any rate
it's odd to see a smiling sunny one, willingness to please those willing to be pleased.
She sticks finger in mouth, presses down her lower teeth, a jiggling quiver
as if nibbling cuttlebone. All our defect, this talking out of season.

Saint Oddseth Visits Gaul

Your peasants are like ours, cloth tube lumped over the shoulders, naked legs
and the churches, of such stone as the locality provides, piebald and whistling
who will to matins, matinward I suppose you'll say, these chalices
tall and narrowshouldered like your houses have (I confess) better wine in
and medallions, one in blue glass fused to the metal, sapphire button
with the Holy Ghost in, beat our footed basons if you like to think it; our
bread is better in a way, wrenchable if you have teeth, your crusts fine, butter
good but dear. I miss our crabs we bash with a rock to get at, boiled
and island waves addressing rock indistinguishable from chapel as if the island's it.
Please hurry copying off these manuscripts. I'll have a case made, fitted leather
with one of those medallions. The Holy Ghost I think's a gull, best as a gull.

Shroud of Turin Postcard

This hologramic postcard of the shroud of Turin
(eyeholes in weave, white space for moustache) alternates
with the soppiest imaginable color haloed Christ
eyes on you with false directness like Olympia's, peering
through the weave, X-ray of itself, Wittgenstein's duck-rabbit
redone has two fold-lines angling up and down, at crown
of the head and beard tip, so vigorous they show a little and
somewhere off to the left meet, framed in radiation, vapor
trail, slug trail. This is not His face, you say, rejecting it
like a dish with brandy in you think they'll overdo
or as if your appetite for religion were too attended to.

Not the Thing Itself but—

And so, thinking about a treasure they go, librarians imagining a lost floor
below A-level with books in dull yet jewel-colored bindings, smell of must
like the sound of foot on cement floor, the light switches fixed to the freestanding
shelves old-fashioned, and in beautifully made boxes on the shelves
manuscripts in minuscule, cherished for the wording, vellum so fine
or coarsely indestructible parchment (barring mouse, beetle, borer) and how is the
point that one might not easily say what something in one bay may not contain,
as Barbara's improbable people in her first line massed by Chichen Itza, itself improbable
chucks us a jaguar's bones like something you'd throw a dog. It is important how a thing
comes to you, provenance not a list of owners (Huth, Widener) but anecdotes
of acquisition. An antler on the chest of drawers in Thompson, curved, cut through,
reminds me in its dryness of a poem's mentioning the charm to stop on the horns cut
in the wrong season bleeding, but this came from the downstairs shed, evicted tenants (so a
slight touch of legal bother clings to it) and the crescent shape it makes, curving
on itself, makes it barely lie flat. I once painted a hollow cow-horn, stuck up on a
paintbrush locked in a dimestore vise, exhibited in a Dallas bookshop as part of the decor.

Work is Speech

"It's time to get our hands dirty," Bruce Andrews says, presumably with Bic
ink. Olson ate the orange garagemechanic cloth in a dream though this is not
always understood. Whitman lauds frisket and tympan and there you are, that "style"
what we think of as style is temporally local. The cuffs on my flannel pajama trousers
have been admired. Praising is what style does, always does, and this requires that style
have a style, and its aristocracy is not (except in grade schools, all hands now vanished into
    sleeves)
to dictate but invite, as Michael Clark with a little bow invites a lion off its perch,
so what is the lion, a capitulation to the brutalizing of getting a living, killing animals and
    vegetables
the necessary accommodation to others we make, speaking to a bus driver
whether so he'll understand or not. Here in Andrews' beautifully lavender *Excommunicate*
words pretty as Spoerri's catsup, wineglasses, crumpled napkins, crumbs, shrimp
are disposed (disponible the French'd say, yours to command, verbal flatware)
and here (again you're wrong, yours to etc. soft, not even sticking to the linen, and verbal
pulled free of *Verbum* in Aquinas, that Lonergan'd study and Gilby translate
a scrap of, the best scrap, we're here at lots of Latin words Andrews has listed (like)
mustardpots standing for field mortars, their place on the page a metaphor, these bib
overalls raspberry as this book, the cut tape stripes meant powerful, and what stays are
    words like parasol,
as if history is knowing the Latin words too.
Vision's workers read, Jack London's lamplit backroom, hobo experiences feeding in
somehow to Cobbett or Sassoon, a difficulty of *finding your way* the experience reading
and experience correct. Ponge kept his labor organizing separate from his florilegia.
To want words charged in their places will surely be like having a notion what use the
Lascars and Malays in Sax Rohmer, fodder of thrills, might come to as this book not quite
the color of revolution *could* go on the shelves of any of our Cambridge bookstores catering
to dissent and not look out of place, aware of itself as horribly different and indeed the

manuals, red books, manifesti promise them a whole intrinsically vulgar relation to reading, the book announcing itself frankly as tool. Let us insert as Spoerri might a stuffed mouse among the shriveling grapes, Sitwell on Bath or de la Mare's *Desert Islands* vandalize the worker's shelf, give him Arabia as if it were the promise of art.

A Crystal Set

Lawyers know that torts are not a class of wrongs;
classes are definable, at least in theory.
Good faith exacted by a title would make a bad poem a tort
say the kind that are a disguised list of things about equally known
to the writer who takes familiarity with everything familiarly
Kipling's lapel button a microphone hearing leopard's name for leopard
his eyes behind thick lenses like monkeys against temple sculpture
poems like that, common knowledge presented as useful. I do like
gusts of gas trailing in fingers like hands made of rusted out roofing tin
from the crossed-wire grid of a mike large enough to compress charcoal grains
no matter which direction, the cab doors lacking inside handles,
hollow sheep half over a stile, clumsy radio inside the belly
figures passing in front of the clock, ribbed one equipped with scythe
say these pass in front of the knobs and warm tubes in the mock sheep
snow coating the left-out porch apple to a globe of snow.

Madox Brown's "Work"

with the "philosopher" tucked in (was Carlyle a philosopher? almost certainly not)
jewellike as its reproductions in the Lond. Mus. exhibit, laborers in an open pit
soil, diggings for gas, Bennett's Riceyman tube collapse, mud slide tunnel's heave
tell us, contemporary, the fact is dreamable, sweet, that which labor labors, is, fact
brutality of subway repair, more dangerous, Mr. Brown's friend Mr. Ross says than Vietnam
large men with hats, bit of beard, cigar and a taste for camouflage attire, wonderful giant
    geodesic windows
impossible to clean, laborer left out of the designer's plans, but here all made well
in the bright Italianate street, sun splashing like children over philosophers in plug hats
discussing that pit men in shirtsleeves rest from the digging of, this delicious stasis
description of a painting pours over it. A Glackens (Kite Flying on Montmartre) I was sent
    as a
postcard, icy greenblue sky, chimneypots, maybe a windmill dissolved in haze, a kite in
    cold air
as if in a balloon of that color says people are less important than kites, air more important
    than people,
painting is important as air. We need spectatorism in a sunlit picture, Bonnard's dog in the
    bathroom,
busyness of tile, not onlooker or connoisseur as in Daumier's series on the man bending
    over portfolios of prints' *pompier*
(Eric Newton's term, un- as he says translatable) but these bearded hatted philosophers
    so sure of knowing

what they know, politicality of economy, how it felt to be medieval as in Van Gogh the
  sower if shod
at all has cardboard brogans paintable as mountains, which opened out are the shape of
  waistcoats.

Double Sonnet for Mickey

In *Kiss Me Deadly* Cloris Leachman asks Mike Hammer in the car Do
you read poetry? He doesn't even answer but just looks at her. The plot
may be said to turn on a book of Christina Rossetti poems but to
me it is that pause, a careless sneer on Meeker's face as he not
only does not answer but sees no reason to get mad. She has no right
to ask the question in the first place of a tough guy whose hair,
just longer than a brush cut, is stiffened by something bryllish that might
ten years before have been brilliantine and he marine rather than air
force straight, chin tending to plumpness suggesting a tight military collar
forsworn. His girlfriend whose chin likewise etcetera gets evidence on johns
in ways not admirable. On the walls of his hideous apartment are camera cases, statues and
  two-dollar
framed people, everyone's limbs pointlessly extended, plasticman fixed for a decade in
  bronze,
none of this inadvert. She asked him knowing he would look at her as if a bad
smell in the car were hers and she, producing it, would know he knew she had.
That look is not eternal. It is a product of the late fifties like *Bucket of Blood,* rude look
at art, snapshot of The Thinker with your sweetheart on his lap and I prefer
another photo of one of its castings blown half apart by terrorists who took
monument for establishment, ecriture for prefecture (how do you deface an Anselm Kiefer,
already glued up with straw and so on?) It's probably the locution, *a* Rodin
that maddened them, one of an oeuvre, thing valued as one of a series of makings
but then it's also celebritous, like the Sphinx now falling to bits, another endangered Man
as Hammer is, in the film made because there first were novels about his undertakings
but then one doesn't recognize a Hammer from sketchiest drawing or collage
the way a sphinx or thinker's fair game for cartoon or cover art. A taste for him is more
like going to the fights, choosing to smell of something that goes with Gillette, massages
a jaw wider than its forehead and thinks of kicking in a green door
behind which shuttered Experience waits, twirling a trilby, trying on a smile
above the angled shoulders built up from folded gauze we thought, then, a masculine style.

The Foreignness of English

The consonants in Edwin Muir listen, bated, for their adjacent vowels
but /it/is/ Alun Lewis rhyming ("All Day it has Rained") or mixing
fours and fives ("Midnight in India" that, a pity, ends in fives, men who
like Christopher Murray Grieve put not always noun to verb but 'n' to 'ou', for
us kohl on the eyelid, for Lewis memory or something like memory of a child scrutting for coal,
Dyment's dueling swans, the dead one leaving down on the water "like children's little boäts"
two syllables in Nova Scotia, as my Scottish grandfather after his stroke would work at

17

finishing a phrase with a word as if it were a syllable. Language is the shape of a thistle,
lots of fine tubes between rose, amethyst, lilac, something mineral inside a flower, and it's
   not the
age of this stuffing but the newness of the new one, true bee vraiment buzzing in French,
la something, Jimenez loving so the assertiveness of Spanish *jo,* the shape
of the wings in some odd kinds of flies reminding us whatever we think a shape is there's
another way to make that shape, as water in the pitcher plant's viol-shaped tum
comes not from the sky but osmotically out of the ground, osmos its cosmos, the
Wellesley greenhouse's empty at Easter, but the Sensitive Plant touched at its tip
collapsed its needles (softer than pine) in pairs sequentially down the stem
retreating like solidest accent from syllables now perceived as having none, Ruth Pitter's
flatfaced woes impossible as cream rising in the milkbottle neck, frozen. Our language
is simply meant to be disposable, winged thing between screen and pane, drying untriste.

Ing Poem for Sheila Murphy

Opening the envelope from Sheila Murphy a pamphlet drops out, the wrapper palest violet
and I'm reminded of one who wrote on mismatched stationery, any spiralbound edge
   ripped from
her heart and folded very small, like a theater ticket or what mindreaders
call a "billet," thing in a corner, the envelope floridly addressed, addressing the
addressee like branding a cow, pain shared, burned hair, the shininess of your name (become
by force of handwriting her name) dredged into paper with cheapest ballpoint, sometimes
the enclosure unfolded was a drawing meant to be her face, most wittily distraught, the
shift of medium from written speech to pen writing a picture, this was writing,
meant to be a letter, which 's to say I believe I was meant to read the face there
as Sheila's flute I've never heard is audible, barely, as a kind of fact behind her poems,
like her gender, thing known and as known perceived, and for these opening your poems
   beginning
Sitting in the mud I washed the teacup with a flattened hedgehog, listening to Mozart,
   wondering
how to make it clear the hedgehog was not the listener though in mien like Berlioz, this
wisdom even animals being used as tuffies have ("comfort oligarchy sponge"). A moulded
   plastic one
my old dog charged would squeak when bit or pranced on and you, flute cocked to lips
I've only seen in dreams know best, bonne bouche, embouche, the trill of practicing.

At Bottom, Gray

That strange feel off France, refrigerant cafés, by simple opposition Au Bon Pain
steaming of a Sunday, the young girls in pink with patent shoes, white socks
battering at each other by the lavatory door, the tile gray near the inside wall,
crimson toward windows. It doesn't matter that the customers speak Finnish
and look just as middleclass as us, Harvard's tiny reddish bricks like picks of a pen,
like leaves. Maybe it isn't Finnish. Maybe they're not middleclass. Street-*volk* attach
themselves at the busiest times to the flushing place for a wash. Sometimes the police
eject one in too long. A silvered shield in the upper outside corner shows anyone

behind the counter what we do. Baudelaire comes in, looking like the little Etonians attending Verlaine

in Beerbohm's drawing, helpfully reproduced by Gaunt (*The Aesthetic Adventure,* Pelican) on the cover-o a

Wilde like Divine in a Spray-Net wig suspicious of the dancer, modernist tarot. A watering can or Dine pliers, wrench,

the other's cast brushhandles in a coffeecan would not be out of place, felt to intrude, all the Goreyans

hoping Captain Hook would commit something predictable. These lovelinesses, a silver snuffbox if you

don't take snuff are comfort in the mood they help create, as Edith Sitwell's rings reminded her she was an Empress and must remember almost all the time to talk like one.

Written in Dejection

The zoos are shut. (It's late.) In San Antonio, tall building of cut stone, mangers
of iron like fireplace racks high up on the wall hold fresh green alfalfa
for the giraffes with spots the color of rusty tan, one very old one so tall
its head is mostly hid though he (is it he? that part's hid too) ducks to see us, lips
in a curve like a rarefied camel, nostril line peculiarly fine, pennine and
the weight of this great neck not braced by great projections at the shoulders
the height of it automatic unless pressed into Barnum's car, surprising the
depressions by the flanks, possibilities for indention, gracile boxiness of all, no
way a gowk. The koala were only incipient but the whooping crane (lent)
sounds like an elephant, snakes green as limes still knot to branches and
attendants in summer tans swill down bearpits, scrub disinfectant in the penguin shelter,
and seem pleased to be where the animals are. Baby anteaters find
their lives probable. Outside, really in the parking lot, a carousel classic in its horses
larger and smaller (some jeweled) and twisty poles down to them are cast resin, the bird
I remember from years ago the exact color of orange sherbet no longer there. Bless
the gibbons' phatic hoot, the wombat asleep upside-down, only the back legs showing,
paws curved like hands or upside-down back legs, and far away but drivable a
Gauguin self-portrait locked in its frame thinks of Detroit where Whistler's "Cremorne
Gardens" that brought the lawsuit with Ruskin isn't locked in at all, the grand
horror of artists' lives occurring for me always in Texas light altering the colors in
Degas milliners' shops, even the cheetahs sitting a little differently on the land.

Two Wind Poems

Sand Alembic

Wind rushing through the gut, it is false
one has to be near the body to reach in,
pull out of it peccant matter, chuck,
invisible in an invisible pail, the vein on my
wrist transverse, uncopyable as blue
penciling on onionskin. A Doughty with its

foldout maps shows desert, djinn area
traveled by people who need no body.
Cities half as old as language listen like
the crumpling of the engraving's tissue.
A circle made anywhere, scribed vacancy
is definable without /prior to/ intention, all
horses and their equipage trapped in a gradually
flattening sphere like Saturn or a lens
till so flat it isn't there, rotation
winking out with volume, quality in that
nonspecifiable instant vanishing with substance,
burglar with plate in a sack, stars glass stuck
in a wall, how large a vessel can be a question
very like the direction and distance of an absent
body intuited. The comb run through hair picks up
fine particles from anywhere. We black the face of our page
to grace the turban but he grows up, his fan a palm.
Entering a room is magic, scanning calendar
for date, inside the putative area
like a fly in a fist.

The Fan

A field in which we look, blankly,
at a *spread* of interest, idle as a
dollhouse interior and about those dimensions,
not even windowbox as farm but
thick monstera stem entering soil in its pot,
what the sun does, shadow on broken ground,
half-focused stare at a corner of the room
not till then a "corner" can be purely
interior, our footsteps in a subway tunnel slowing,
stop as a past action usually recent arrests
us like the framed ad for the largest bookstore ever or
occult paraphernalia, these spots indeed in which
the attention wanders in place connect us to
those animals in fields we're to emulate, unclad
and chewing, some wind in our hyacinthine
spill of mane, those eyes too, Napoleon
on Alp exclusive for the nonce of ways and means,
this marble (if I had one) rolling idly on
the desktop or still, thing for Alex
Troup to build into a wee crate, shredded
paper, an old bottle empty of its cork
the discard racing away from us which we acknowledge, like some red
shift by the blankness with which we attend to the
possibility of perception, form of forms, for which no
words exist or are appropriate, wedge of world we've
selected prior to interest.

Punk Bilingual Satanists

eat people in Matamoros, making me wonder if blood
sacrifice is unknown in (say) San Antonio, full of
dears, it not enough argument that being abductable
for slaughter loopy, ersatz, impromptu (it takes commitment
and application to become a *brujo,* for the other merely
half-remembered Christianity and a liking for effect, say
an upside down black cross dangled from an earlobe)
or how nice that sex is not the sole reason any more,
so daughters, sons friendly pickup trucks want to eat your brains—
the people on the loose attractive, healthy and so
one close to me says you can't tell the devil. A new book on Crippen bears
his caricature, weak watery but not unfriendly eyes, frond moustache
but then he was as it were presented with his victim. The difference may be
that killing for ritual inducts you into a sect willy nilly, like
stuffing a mattress with part of your hair, the truck
announcing that it transports sleep. Oh one is altered
by evangelical belief, the soul ripped temporarily from body
not, probably, sent as emissary but at best exemplariness,
proof the others have done a wicked thing, that there are people
who always will, not instrumentally, to achieve something, to
alter a relation, not grasping what they grasp, not doing
evil enough, more like peeling a paper label from a can of soup,
thing to be about, picking at the patches of hard glue, a
triviality, external, and the soup itself only eaten to have eaten.

Metaphysics

Reading Pieper I had this dream (rather than vision) of
Orson Welles as Aquinas, saying in accents wry as if French
"It comes down to mystery, mystery. Imagine that the world is understood,
can you then say the world is understood?" universe his glass ball, or
Schell interrogating Dietrich, what's true, the wonderful cheek planes
at any age, like the walls of his mockup of her apartment, place in
which to pretend to situate an event recorded elsewhere. The
gold hair in this oval locket *isn't* Byron's, but is to be taken as
(like the lady's Quennell describes, wrapped in paper, her name forgot,
"some woman off Leghorn") his ostensively, the assertion theatrical,
understood as a possession at a time of Byron's even if we made it yesterday
this this Byron's was. Impact or proximity excite, striking adjacence
and not a thing disposable, Dickens's razors not his suds. To be bowl
and stick is property of history pretending to be philosophy, soap figure of
Voltaire you rub daily on the way to the sink till he's bald, wigless
yet still a sophe. Intend the world and it will seek you out
folded napkin through bone ring, the pendant glass in facets, stuck carelessly
in a stick ditto, become a spectrum as good as Newton's on the stairway wall
and as always I looked for the brown part, unable even to imagine where on
the light smear it would be, and Galileo in another room imagines a sphere
of welded metal plates, deathstar, with a characteristic hokey sound of its own

to show the space it occupies is strained around it, and it's no matter, as
Williams says a dishmop bound in copper is everything, bearer of
light, a scum of silver paperclips and unfolded silver folding scissors
in a shaving bowl the same metal, whatever that metal is, Welles
present by assertion only not in any of its reflections but the sum of them.

Against Interruptions

Leave me alone, you fools, the mad scientist says
having become invisible or animated a limb—we
respond to it, throatily, from Claude Rains
or its nostalgic shadow in some midperiod Hammer
as if we too had known more than the prefect, burgomaster
(ably played, perhaps with a monocle, by Atwill)
so in a flash we see beyond his crystalline stare
The Work, strenuous application of mind to flesh, wax, the
choice and force implied in Tesla switches, unpatented
the measurings of Mr. Hyde producing, later, Crippen.
It's the aftermath, bodies everywhere, that make it seem a bit like war
but we vote beforehand for the Doktor who knowing what he wants
has equipment to order, victims to solicit or exhume, that same
batch of crystals, you know the ones, with a fortuitous impurity
like his, stain on the soul almost indistinguishable from learning.
Leave us alone, we say, to those who want our films like theirs
the travelogue, market town, old millpond without the kirtled
evidence that something we made up's amiss, dripping daisies.

Without Sitting Down

Mozart wrote as if his hand should always float, be above
coming down as definitive, bad for the hand as he said of some people's
composition for teaching it to perch. Angels on viola
and cello have bows like each other, stretched like spearthrowers
or device to test wagonwheels for true. Yet the hand is
not a bird unless everything is, those pin-pipestem bones, the word *aile,*
blade of an oar cut over winter, hand rubbing over its edge the way
carpenters have, sanding with the palm's lines, bit of moisture and oil reacting to grain.
Lift the palm always, be ready to leave the made thing, leave the phrase, the composition
to work itself out, unladen by its composer, of mannered performance so
much ownership, as Beerbohm suggested, having lived into the essence of your subject,
letting it discompose, pupate, necessary stage in which you can't see
or dictate what will go where, Henry James a gradually fixed form, the
whole body a comment on the oblong fierce head, bent finally over hotel shoes, his, hers
as if you don't rest but the drawing does, pigment in suspension darkening near a thicker
edge, no cheating like the angel reflection milked out in glass overlay
knowing in the sense of acting on that you never have to come down,
only graphite and green-blue, on the shoe.

Mould Like Silk

His nouns have pain in them. It's like a farm you suffered on till
every rise of land, barbed-wire dump (no, that's his listing)'s so
saturated with sorrow you leave—his paper match *skates* in
the urinal, the shadows below the bridge as much the bridge to him,
hobo pockets. Anyway that impetus, that feels like Browning crossed
somehow with topographical poets, Grongar Hill—turns from
his feeling something when looking at . . . that in a way this blaze
without smoke is like pretending the black chimney remembers flame.
We keep looking at our watch. A bubble at the high point of the lens reminds us
of things like it. Forget them. Mould jello in a soup plate with one grape.
Oh any animal may have a *sleek* head, dormouse out of pot,
the lid a knobbed cap. Officiate like some conductor, show us
Winter Garden, Navy Yard, places known better by report, meek Marianne
apostrophizing Roebling. There's no harp here if we don't lie, thing you'd say
if you don't play a stringed instrument, especially fretless. It's not a subject,
unless those boring geometricals in stretched thread the other highschool made
were interesting, when even colored against black they weren't, the
polygon itself, base shape, almost promising in dusty light the same as fell
on sport trophies, those figures supposed to be Greek with basketballs glittering
and a plate to say what year it was exciting. That one can walk
partway across, the footing uncertain, is like the photographs of Kramden in the Raccoon
     Lodge
sharing the murk with tarpon, anything furry stuffed, thing dusty
on a shelf, bridge dusty yet ensanguined, "orphic strings," its current nets like
clouds of thinking, the slightly sooted cobwebs that, touching white drainpipe fascia
cling to it forever like an allusion unaccountably hard to wipe off.

Angoes of Mancles

The mind half-silvered admits or reflects like flipping
a coin, rewriting north to south, sun moon's angry candy, just shift
and let the old epithet stand, no doubt on dolphin feet, since they
haven't. The poem's dimpled as if with rain from this idiot
distressing of any surface, the highlight on the nose provoking
Cézanne to comment, "like a bed-knob!" each so predictably with it.
Here is a stamp showing an Indian pot (I haven't one
but they're common.) The pattern is like quillwork, the quill a
substitute for plastic. One begins to digitize bird feathers
for beads to render, more violent than the mice I saw
in a lace hem, a keepsake, as the checkerboard staggers to split
into curves, the Marilyn quilts. If words in poems are either
on-off the line's patched from choices the extremist happens
to have made, shimmer of hexagonal black and white tile
making patterns where the eye happens to fatigue, designer snakeskin
cow jumping over the sun, as one Harvard bandsman would say,
foul, nasty, British and short, a word changed, see, from Hobbes.

Shaving the Beard

A face like a pillow twisted in illness
is what I see, lumpish, and the lower half
(which after all was hair) more Scottish, the
mouth strange, and like my brother's, twenty-
three years evading by moustache and beard
an approach to age, cheek contour (I've put
my glasses on to see the page clearly) and think
of poets describing parental reflection in bathroom mirror
—what's Stafford's "my father's eyes were gray" to this
hazing like successive Berryman dustjacket shots,
vanity of those alcoholic writers bending to describe
the cherry in the sidecar. Och it's like
throwing a plaid over your business suit, charging tanks,
defoliating countries my ancestors knew, tussling the way
colors do in vertically striped flags the French made
fashionable, or poems in series, the new *Spring*
and All little reprint, so few lines per page the
poems leap out and you hardly see the prose at all.

Light versus Air

From the "Goat Skull and Bottle" we proceed backward to Bonnard,
reflecting fruit in a horizontal mirror; what light does or need do
the difference between limpidity, the soupy summer lake, and fluxal
rayons. Do I wish light to lie as on whitely greenish indented leaf, leaf
in reverse, intaglio not so much the issue as cool opaque concavity to take
light sluicewise, or at least allowing for an overflow, or that which
a la dandelion, wants anywhere elsewhere, escaping substance. To be an end
radiates diffused, slams against. Watercolor furs and fans till you get
to Nolde's "Islander," horizontal stripe across the eyes thin as Green
Lantern's trendy mask, the car parts on the wall wrapping in on
themselves but only Christo's laced oblong parcel in oldest wheelbarrow
a match (for revisioning of self) for Picasso's goat, Balzac and oh a
lovely Lipchitz wrapped in plastic held efficiently with olive packing cellophane tape
because they're sandblasting the stairs or something below, heaped grit, sanding discs
and here an absolutely standard aluminum cylinder with ashtray top, exactly
half the butts corktips, one pulled almost to orange
by the red of lipstick half its length and in front a hole makes it a guitar.

Surfaces are Points

The archetype of a seal would be its ectype in reverse, blood-filamented jasper
wandering through itself, direction disguised as diversion, du jour.
Government leather holsters, cartridge belts, binocular cases are designed to wear
     criss-cross,
the world full of effigies with hollows where stone eyes were lost or, not lost,
without the pupils fitted from a different stone, focus of a mosque a niche of fitted tile.
Sponges and cowries must be dried, before they can be worn, or sponginess applied.
Reed rods ending in metal sleeves to take a natural quill need a finial or bezel
to balance one's imagination. Bases, podia, survive their objects, frontal gryphon pedal
     herm the
dream of being supported by servants. Collander top to charcoal fire would throw
galaxies on painted ceiling Marses in Scorpio. Any decor at all, the least ornament, rafter
joints of tied bamboo, resemble the cheese sandwich cut from the corners in an X, making of a
doughy square twelve points.
Canonicize this pun that diminishing extremities concentrate. The pig with spear in
is not running out pig through the pole, the knife
through the painting not sapping its virtu.

Tombeau d'Edgar

is white stone, very carvable, Virginia's side panel with four puttied holes
where, one supposes, a plaque was, since carved with her name, her mother's
the other side and Edgar's, the most weathered, 09-49, and way off behind
everything an odd flowerbed with stone with raven on (Nevermore), original
site before they moved them all, Baltimorean schoolchild pennies saved for
what was it before extensive restoration (bronze medallion '86, a French
gift under lucite for an original bronze tribute, urban archeology
layered like detection. No mention of Mallarmé, or dedication absentees
whose names roll less readily off the tongue. It's hilly, Baltimore,
with High and Low streets near its shot tower out by Albemarle. The city
was in its way hospitable, oysters, cotton, Betsy Ross's stylish little house
like the Two Bad Mice's. What signs of anyone, monocled Joyce in
Motherwell's etching wearing its tint, Harvard acquires 109 original leaves
of Boswell's Johnson, Manet's monocled gentleman accessible, and
a Chinese bronze cylindrical box reproduced, square hole in the center
like money, tiny spout, for ink the salesperson says, to mix, store or pour out ink.
Bunch of flowers on his tomb, held back with a black ribbon, the petal I saved
a deep red-purple, already stiff from being in my pocket.

Spinous Protuberants

Grotesquerie—jagged outlines in copper we mistake for the sea serpent—
makes possible armadillos of shredded truck tires, slugs in the bathroom merely marks
on walls, old tape, half the mermaids we see which merely start a green near
spine end. That anything *can* be anything else needs no proof when anything over the arm's

a cane, black ribbon a rose, crumpled tissue (as Ponge would say) carnation, the
attribute galloping toward substance. Jimenez the ultimate acrylic sculptor
screws red bulbs into candyflake horses' eyes, Barbara Jordan ends a poem with
fish swimming through aquarium skull apertures, the feel
of watching this thinking as little of fish as our mortality, a garland
looked at, something for the darkgreen tin cornucopiae ending in spiky rods
sold around Memorial Day, their color meant to blend with circumambient leaves, an
architecture trumpet like the Wall to walk around, in theory, feel the sorrow
flowers feel, litter of deathday cookies worn as medallions, a necklace or the
lindenwood beads like a vertebrate tail, each a Germanic Christ on one side
the other a skull extremely stylized, we thought an oddness from not having only that
in a pocket or stuck through the belt like a little whip. My hand is a cup
for your hand, cupped cups, nothing at all any more interior.

Words for Bronze

Nuevo Laredo, not home of hippies but ordinary people like those around
my house in Dallas, for whom thin aluminum pots replaced museum-quality
portrait and stirrup-handled jugs, one in San Antonio of a named young woman
breasts and face hieratically eager, a kind thing like allusion to put up
the popular in clay, the glaze like heavy soy oil over French vanilla, presence like
Quatrale's holloweyed ram in Boston. No museum tour these bottles of vanilla,
beltbuckles and -tips matched German silver in sidewalk and shop, doorstop plaster
everythings, adzed St. Francis advertised at $200, next door selling
birdcages of all heights, welded wire. Mostly the signs all in a foreign tongue
dragged the eye as neon might in Kyoto. A circle of tall stones made me think they make
stelae again, electric lamps or stumps high up there, around a Fountain of Poets named
for a sonnet in perfect hexameters. I plunged my hands in to the wrist.
The fountain in the poem is a metaphor. It mentions all the qualities that might apply
to water blubbing up (and over rims) on a hot day, artichoke with a pipe stuck up it, halved
    melons.

To Paul of Saint Victor

That it is there beforehand may be proved by his reported habit of scattering
pretty words on a page as Chaplin distributes grain to the poor man's progeny
as if they'd peck, the more precise acknowledgement that tissues have nodules because
    they are tissues,
not necessarily nouns but qualities, nominal as perceived against a ground. This child
    clapping
hands and gurgling like a pigeon is like Glück's acknowledging the fact that words are
    world, in
a sense. The traum of idleness sections from the All a field, as if a quilt, rugs on seagreen tile
islands by that accident, Tissot's embattled infant's admiral's hat a periodical, her
gelid confection mountain to insurgent cream. One tends to describe once an area has been
    defined

as if attention drying like a sea leaves Waco. We occupy as a frontier the beginnings of
moisture—the
house we occupy has a picture of waves, the biggest of them backlit to transparency, effect
shot for
on angel wings and Delacroix's peccant swimmers, till Monet's *dark* squiggles on light
water.
Recently I got to check Manet's "Railroad Station" in our National Gallery. Her open
book scribbled
on in luminous gray *is* a railway timetable (or an almanac), not the verse a wag suggested
because the book, though thick, is folded only once and sewn. Some questions even about art
can be answered. The humid eyes of Greuze leave one less occupied than Fragonard's dry
women playing semiclad, indelicate, with dogs painted with light, moist strokes.
It doesn't really say that everything is paint, any more than the omnilegent's words fading into
lines are meant to retain, as handling, their Alexandrian occasions. Phatic child battering
with fingernail rigidest leaf of American Airlines magazine, ambience of that which you
attempt to decorate, the uninventive randomness of bored play is key (as we approach
O'Hare, haze
pallid over Illinois) that more is needed, generosity of meaning, as the barn owl's
dish-shaped face collects
evidence of mouse or we, moved by the backlit bat, tremble at the frugivorous.

The Red Widow

Carr called it, two upright grooved struts and a weighted blade in a wood chock you'd
pull a cord releasing same to sever noble vertebrae, ours now
for the bureaucrat in his mockserge suit and stickemup tie, palest yellow with lozenged spots
he'll have to loosen. In the rack a Hockney retrospective poster, reticulated wavelets
as one in a red blazer muted to cool observes the pool, museum rectangle,
swimmer's flesh dulled down to muddy greeny gray elbow to knee, och
to see oursel's in management loafers while the workers (four million more in '89)
put out 13 percent more work . . . these economic patterns weave
o'er that which drowning learned to wave, its English cousins' safetypin
earrings bitterness's panache. What saves it all is that it's clear,
museum-cool, a medium; mere description hypnotizes like a myth.
In the same rack the young Alfonso or whoever he is in a red suit
has caged birds and one on a lead cord watched by rotund Tenniel cats.
Images may still arrest but lack the thirties-poster power, bayonet
through the backwardbending worker an event in graphicland, a "visual"
to show if we weren't there and can't remount the genuine event.

Blowing Down Flats

Adam, Eve squabble in an iron box with windows that rings like an oildrum eating a radio,
echoic
value to remembered quarrels as theater, "Two Gentlemen" set blown down last night in
Dallas, the newspaper

picture all purple showing spots behind the columned valance, "Security officer Rick
    Woolverton" in a yellow slicker
reflected in a pool below himself, above lightning like chalk or beansprout roots, mole
    whiskers, coming
down to angle up again, parabola not reflected in what the picture chooses to show,
    electrical effects
outlasting wind. In a day or so the tank parade will go on as planned. Such energy
over even this cuted up Shakespeare stage (now folded) is what one imagines him imagining
always in the back the Kid all white with a blue sash, lisped sententiae, next generation's
    principal,
yesterday's show similarly wrapped up, the experience of the actor so different in this respect
from what the public sees, last season's tights' residual gray at knees. Oh it concentrates
    the mind, a
stage decked with lights under boards like decks, the motives candles might show in the
    space after dinner
the sky your scrim, this dog my dog, bandaged aerialists on battered wagons parade
(verb) to the new stage (noun) lit by lights (noun) that are truck headlights aimed all in, we tear
from the iron ball of our indifference a performance riveting as the nose of an aluminum canoe
stuck through a curtain may announce itself as a submarine, a staff reglued with silver band
    to hide the join
and booke, if only a sheaf of Churchill telegrams ripp'd from their frames, his presence a
strong inference from the fat cigar in its silver cradle over a silver tray. Like a Camel packet
folded to make a pyramid, the interference from another level is how you gauge intention has
designs upon, attention. Think on this (click) then on this. Always choose the lead. In a less
Pickwickian sense those who "picked up their lawn chairs and blankets and headed for
    their cars" saw the whole play
Verona and Venice kind of similar in their minds.

The Wish to Believe

led William James to vacant hours in seance rooms, medium's cabinet's curtains
billowing out (Marjorie's did) and a cold wind on the hands flat on the table, fingers
to wrists, Houdini's tourniqueted leg sensitive to Marjorie's tendons, ankle motion and
the bell box rang, impressing committeemen more willing to hope a doctor's wife
preserved from hoax (Bostonian) by her gentility. The Tichborne claimant, picked up (he
    said) by sailors at sea,
took a London court four months to fault. Those who pull diseases out of patients' bodies
show the knot or nubbin like a walnut or washer-dryer bolt. Any object is proof, surely
that there are objects, docketed items and an eyeglass on Price's table; had the Bethesda
    pool been sand
it could be photographed after. One might wish to believe in clues without crimes for
the soul's health, live quiet, inoffensive (one argued that the innocent generate nemeses.)
    Purity
is indifferent to outcomes. The bougainvillea flower watered or not, rotating in their pots in
    wind
because the sprays extended to catch the sun make sails. Rotated on a pedestal
they might remain symmetrical as a teen in a prom gown all justice and tulle.

Heritance

Such property as birds'-nest caves and honey-trees
may be divided among all the children.
—Charles Hose, *Natural Man: a record from Borneo*

That we keep. There are poets (such as Jim Haining) for whom keep, have, even for
are nouns, relations become nouns, as before fronts, a bit truculently, after, Harvard
Alumni Gazette's personal narratives or Creeley in the Senior Common Room feeling back
to the Bick, or in the Master's enameled den out of place. I remember Brower's edition
of Pope's Homer, not a thing to touch there as one thought on Broome or Brome,
the fine points of pipe and slipper scholarship. Walking away on uneven brick, the smell of cat.
Widener smells of buckram and sizing, despair of those wanting to be another Wolfe—Harry
Austryn Wolfson, H. A., met in the stacks, agreed Maimon should be translated (suggesting
    me), me awed
by those expert in Crescas and Spinoza, able to say if he were ultimately pantheist. The
    proof is neat.
Imagine Milton sitting in a garden, ideally Longfellow's, feeling an armillary sphere while
    daughters plain
yet elegant read him Tasso in Italian, not Fairfax. One of them looks like Stevie Smith
and will not have the daughter for whom Johnson writes the prologue, the sort of scenario
Ms. Woolf imagining daughters might generate, one wondering if the bee trapped in metal
    hoops
about to penetrate the ecliptic might not, unscared off by his lace, light on cuff or wrist
and if so whose intelligence it would be directing to this fault, if fault it be. The diffidence
of her perception is like what it was to be at Harvard then in '58 or '60, '62.

Mounted Pincer

The mango's improbably large kernel resists cutting as if an
avocado seed were the size of a handball. Xylem in the tree
generates cork around the picture (anecdote deserving rest), a sheep
riven of speciation crawling over fields, exuding ichor. Hughes's
boot presses against soil, the rope taut, wire loop in the uterus
engaging neck, arched windows of some fenestrated Stonehenge shardless
in no moon, what's just inside the skull, under the pia mater
thickening aptly to dream of density, the myth Resistance
like something in Keats out of the ground, clangy monolith, that which
we piecing through at the end pick over, some Salvation Army cufflink
bar, a wee bit bent, flipped through its shank slow-quick, slow-quick,
flat from the cuff's starch against embroidered hole. Whizzing
whir of cicada rising without cutoff, the mind is a killing-bottle
some carbon tet in wool the resident genius. No glebe without
its plow, fen without fairy lantern, jack fool in bog
and fox and fop intersect in glen, wings of these fairies not goss-
amer but thick and hard as a walnut shell, gnurled ochre.
If you stand under a bridge and listen to the water there
it tells you there'll be fire ants if you sit. Untenanted, a fly
or two above, you know fierce worms with jaws like steamshovels
wave like lilies and eat anything that falls in, even pollen.

Water is Fire

That apparent parthenogenesis sometimes entails scrotal pockets in the female of
    degenerate males,
not much larger than their spermal function, is proved. The bladderwort or duckweed
seems by having invented gametes to have invented gender, hence midi verse's
valiant allegiance to woman as if loyal as if to cause, the cause as personal
as well as drakes eating the weed, and this goes back or is prefigured in the
original ocean's soupy choice of clockwise versus counterclockwise skew in
the amino acid. Oft times we hear of sexless beings in the woods, du Maurier's
wicked elflike dwarf, the sound in early texts of eft. We take what strikes us
vividly as myth as myth, find true what resonates, as pity (and ex nihilo creation,
says Gilson) descend to us from scripture. Belief believes its syntax, hologramic
crucifixions, Jesus on linen Veronicaesque, enough that the world has aspects
for us to take the clot of blood in eggs as evidence though it looks like nothing so much
as the dye capsule in wartime sexless margarine the act of squeezing warmed.

Flasks of Wave

The insight of Sir Thomas Browne that everything is contained in something, the
audible listening as to (not the sound but) the echo of stone in well, Valéry's
remark that a musical tone, the orchestra tuning up, installs a *univers*
demands of us not more theory but less, not harpings on the oceanic feeling
but what it is (is it) twenty-six young men bathing means, that bodies and water
though separated by a pellicle are after all the same, barring salinity and lymph,
that nearness of adjacents is in a sense possible, Eakins's rock our rock, that
even a person in a gas chamber is a group or insects under vacuum, the
body fluids desiccated, heap of snow in bottom of the tube, will mostly return
when broken with a hammer as if their soul is the rose in alchemical experiment, that
which is evoked, or evocation an operation one performs, the
pressure of one at the window, peering through miniblinds at the street, repairing to
the bathroom, where a toiletpaper holder *no longer* is but with its screws
in a rectangular plastic basin, in the kitchen, under the sink's under
a bulky Chemex flask, has the grain of anything beginning to await its fate, in
the next bin over, really under the sink, bent pipes are the sound of horns,
leavetakings, confetti of dust on white, dead white plastique shelf liner fitted
over a crack in boards themselves white, this little room from which one might see
through filigree oh, legs of one busied at the sink, in which a square plastic basin
from Holland, very white, functions as a remark, like the white plastic or plasticized
drain strainer we saw, its holes like holes, central knob shiny black
to let a matte black rubber circle down to hold water also, la to its mer ici.

Old Images

To end abetting the tyrant, striped dishclout on ceramic pig's head over faucet,
the eyes wholly enigmatic over circular nose, cloth not caring what it's draped on, pig without
knowledge of woven babushka, there's this import given the lump of cold white porcelain
or cloth, not "knowing" les autres, kitchen grotto indifferent in kind from pieced della Robbia
in Baltimore, whole Garden of Eden with tree, snake fat and human-headed, pale
Adam, pale Eve, some vulnerability as a sculpted group, parts of each other,
glazed knot, the snake's head for some reason discounted, in its ambivalence like fruit.
Meaning is kindly, behovely, and this does not mean (means not, some, any archaism) evil
does not float, merely as a nondescript set of points, not even attracted by good
as a cloud to an updraft, deliberate archaism an archaism, the wicked a gift
cold as a lake bottom, scaled, we know has a human face, Saxon yaft
thinking back to a selfishness in giving, guarding "treasure," rings of iron or cheap jade.
We don't want the treasure so much as an evil proportioned like ourselves, Industrial
Light & Magic shaping seawater into our features, hence the lion or gorgon gushing water
even if, unpiped, a bezel on a Renaissance table, Lir's head on bridge over Liffey like
    Napoleon's N
any lump or cloud we make any shape we see in, bunned hair around the serpent's face
whatever's fashionable, indifferent to gender, prior to mating but always, like the stone pig
or dolphin, poised for some act we only begin to imagine.

The Poet's Office

[for John Herndon]

An age "daft after great figures," Nicolson remarks of Tennyson's,
albums titanizing fleur, Arcadian Farewell, bishops with the manner of ministers
(Holmes to his Irregulars a kind of god), crop's carbuncle blue against bluewhite skin
like the shadows on snow, like one's dead sister, and how as he says they settled into the part
often as not, Francis Newman under dark carving, batwings folded, for Raoul
a smirk, master of makeshift, the grotesque his crime, and its daughter the picturesque,
toffeecans with birds like the cover of *Nature*. Infinite pamphlets I got to catalogue
on sewage treatment (and disestablishing the Irish Church) the same kind of thing, new
application of efficiency to problems posed by numbers, as the Ripper was perhaps a remark
that there were too many, so they stood giant in cloaks "come to stand for something
the poet is assumed to have, inscrutably other," pleasant to find in Ross's *Failure of*
    Modernism it
ending "A Chain for Madeleine," swathed as if in bronze by such material
folding over them like a knee or linenfold carving in darkest oak setting off matched
apostle spoons, Durante exiting in graded pools of light, a way of being medieval.
Not optics but athleticism, Keaton in the rigging himself a sextant.
What you see up there's a prospect, forty counties with sheep like mites in cheese (they also
say, though real infestment's harder to import) and we're back to Newman, zany,
gnawing the cardinal's ankle. Our tweeds and thick-strap Birkenstocks mark us
like buckles on hatbands as advocates of odd agenda, some singularity
allowed us, liking one's job signs xeroxed to death, figurine on viewing screen, smart aleck
    cup.

Reviewing Todd

It's true, Ms. Kemp, *Return of the world* as reviewed's twisty as a twist tie
on bagged fruit, heft of plum, stupid oval of canteloupe, larger than a human
brain, tunneling through his difficult and staggered verse line, apparently
shapeless mountain barrow for encapsulated freight. I once asked
how we know the bicycle's not a natural form, banana or geode stuck with pale
purple crystals. These spokes could have grown in Darcyan expansion
giving birth at the rim to rubber. I write you with a sense that there's a dignity
to be kept up, reminding myself as if a reply to a random prompt of Virginia's
dead-accurate *Marginalia* in which Poe did Conning Tower squibs like F.P.A.
all about literature, intelligibility, on the opacity of texts, Sale's *Koran,* French
Baudelaire read as feuilletons, bleus, pneumatics of literature in Manet's Paris
one thinks of using drive-in banks's whuffy shunts. Baron's poems are a pleasure
because you thumb the catch and a word or phrase, held together like one of David
Searcy's lap joints by guess and god damn falls out to be unfolded, just
a receipt, printed even, how you get it romantic as Stevenson, writing come in a bottle
and what I say's you don't rip open such a thing, throw the envelope away
much less sit down to answer it. The jogger (really a walker), our neighbor Dixie, wears
wrist weights. If our dog hadn't got us up when the alarm failed we'd not have known.
It's child's play to make fact relevant, invoking its airspace, following the voucher
number to a gap, bringing the poem (or phrase) to a close. Barbara Smith wrote a
book about that. Letters are messages, meant rather than intended, letters returned to
the world as one lets a small animal out found in the house, Thoreau's furniture
incipiently lawn. If one were very dense though exactly the size one is one
would swim through limestone, gasp in the cave's bubble, cling to granite as an
unchanging element and this could be written up but not as a postcard
for Pandemonium, experiencing indigestion in angel diners, the seat too soft, one's
writing unassimilable, as Poe said bursting into flame at touch of pen, nue (is it, with an e)
from being la, ostridgean thing waving in some silly pantomime, Caesar and
Cleopatra still performed at Minsky's, the sausage phallus, emperor's bicycle.

Lithops

are little cacti, leaf-succulents, which imitate whatever size they are clusters of
greeny-gray rock, often appearing translucent, and from the similarity of shape
that mutually cognizant orientation crystals have when they make room
for each, growing out of, deposited on, each. For all I know it's Lithops is
as one speaks of an organism in general, the species as itself the animal
familiar, as if on a first-name basis with worm, diatom, a lecture-habit
maybe as old as Linnaeus. You could think of the old Scots in Edinburgh
inventing chemistry referring so to oxides, range of lithiums, ph in sulphates
imperial decor, hindoo, its diagramed, pointlessly enclosed ellipses, each
a sphere. Property becomes an ownership when not all can understand
the proofs in courses all must take, and we are funded behind wee cacti
with spinous asterisks by emerald made by flush of pink over mineral flesh of a sort,
assorted in tiny boxes, cheap-pressed black or white plastic, littered on top with vermiculite-
like gravel like when they are small the none or few cactus chips themselves, savers
of water, come the card says from South Africa, comparable to hairy-old-men phalli
and these others that send up a foot or so from tiniest green rosette a feeler,
waving slightly in the air conditioning.

For Preliterates

regarded by all as political compost, the obscure companies
now want you to rise on Shelleyan wings if it's wings one
rises on, to comprehend as your slipshod dialects won't and can't
but can't only by refusal, the gift—a thing *you* give—of precision
as you might hold a baby, its center of gravity your center, hominid thumb
bracing emergent shoulder, forefinger under nucal spine, you *could* do this
with literacy, test through the math, give *value* daily where lunchtime joint (the
lunchtime joint in Auden) holding sway, note here uncertainty of language
that, as Bateson says in *English Poetry and the English Language*
requires two words (or workers) where one will do, inscribes on the wrapper
around your sandwich (when *was* newspaper last used) messages you know from
packaging inessential, at present advice from famous coaches on milk our notion
of future, fund of readers safely skipping the articles of *an, a* describing their condition
as absolute, predictability in any case the matrix since Grant, since Ford,
belied by fact relayed, by no necessity, in news that if it speaks to us
compels a taste for chat, and the verb used a little wrongly as in Hart Crane
and should we ask you to read Crane, the equivalent in content to Bridges'
Testament of Beauty when it's uppity to leave you, like public parks
places you won't go, repair to for crime or eat prefabricated chicken in?
Cast-iron grills and sewer plates have, traditionally, names on eked out by stars,
panthers, logos like Elizabethan companies that lived above as families
as you are kept below by a *taste for* revolutionary texts as much as not, ideology that
for which you opt, lead Marx's spindrift gaze in Highgate sacred to me for Coleridge
descending in his kneesocks the hill to the druggist, the anomaly of giving up
poetry to live in thoughts of poetry.

This End Up

Encouraged by Rauschenberg cardboard-box constructions flat as if
run over, with markings like real markings, see this poem announce
its own orientation as you recognize mother, job, the situation auf ding
or something, as if Herr Batchelder's male child we wanted named Heinz
because such a good name for a post-expressionist painter were art of a sort,
the crosswords'd say, sorted for us with the imagining of it reduced in the Art Book,
there *for* us there, in just that sense inapprehensible, escaping
like politics or paint for the fences around worked-on sewers
with ribbed tubes from noisy compressors (There's a title, Noisy Compressors) that
foppishness of Public Works, yellow Ahabs, orange vests over teeshirts waving us on.
There's things to care about, Lambert's *Music Ho!* and Tippett broadcast pieces on the
state of,
as one reads books on Mozart without listening to him, so the Egyptian one's a surprise
in spite of Hockney's obelisk stage set, Forster on Alexandria, *Tragic Sense of Life* in Flitch
(Dover, bought for a quarter, the cover loose), *Raindrops and Volcanoes, The Web of Life,*
histories
that's to say of how things relate coming to displace Hecht's autobiography, T. E. Lawrence,
Wollstonecraft
and George Sand (*Lelia,* on a bet, beginning why George Sand), Woolley's Bronze Age,
Pirenne

on Medieval Cities, the Wandering Jew, even *Ritual to Romance* with a Baskin cover and
    Bettelheim's *Symbolic Wounds*
to this day an issue, meritocracy having got us to immobility, purely formal interest in
    ideas, unlike
the 17th century on vestments (he of the life of Hazlitt's best first book), even the 19th on
    Infant Baptism
preferable, a certain slippage of concepts, though it multiply adjective, helpful to cosmologists
the tear down the infant's cheek the product of factors, a many Scots come to watch frontier
    station shops
like *Prester John,* empires the product ultimately of their whim and depressions in Paisley,
    no political
import visible at first in ware, niches for knishes. What's supposed to inflame us now is
    abortion
and religious training in the schools. It's quiet because 6:30 chimes. There is a regret for
    regret
in Shallow, luces dripping down his shirtfront, hanging from his points because, in that period,
an extremity of any kind was to make more pointed, theology gathered under triple "heads"
    a field of pikes
because in a way religious wars were no longer fought, less urbanly directed, lettered
    neighbors raising
hues about your rood, the pleasant assumption that everything is a face, thing you countenance
crystallized as anecdotal history, covenanter in the furze bushwhacking bishops, the agents
    of bishops.
To put them on a par by calling them aspects, as if ordering systems put in train are following
    orders,
goes back (fans out) to those thousands of secondrate minds in unspeakably mossy
    rectories
penning sermons later printed, the taste for having a taste for established under tin roofs
laughed at by lead ones brown as owls, the others sheltering Donald Davie to write his
    books on Pound,
purity of diction and syntax, reverend critics and historians yet recognizable, in time, by
    tweed and jeans.

Years of Study

are in the classic acceptation a luxury spent on a medium, the reading of rival texts, devout
attention to echoes of text in the mouths of dogs and cats, finding seasons or beauty of any
    kind, even ideas
quotations, the idle reference a reference, after sawdust and oystershells bridges like harps
mouthed likewise, odor of literacy like bitterness in zucchini. I've a Boynton cup
saying THE BIG CHEESE with wee mouse within, holes like maps of the Gold Mountain
    in broken rectangle,
nine-to-fively counterfactual. It's no mistake, innumerable beeves, hypocrite lector the
    glowing head etched
by Manet, the rhyme of any head casting about it invisible on the page a haze
like a lakelet struck with warm air, off what it seems emitted from, this light discarded by
amateur perception cast off by style, so much itself a summation of what's too delicate for
memory's grabby hand. Our munchkin fervor scorns Mickey's glove (its lines carpalian
    ribs, unparallel).

There isn't, may not be, not even in hobbies, in the protoliterate that sense of starting *lines*
    of investigation
so Henry's private life, Elizabeth's, solidified by Colin Clout and Shakespeare's emit a
    haze of Bacon like mist
in a graveyard, the Mallorcan study by Graves of George Sand (reacting to Catholics) in a
bright yellow cover a slight foreignness of paper, that sense like Stein of quarrels
overlaid by brute perception redeeming the genteel, thin pocketwatch from Seiko saying
    UT or VERITAS
round because hands revolving are, immersed in mercury reclaimed from fish (the fact
    unearned
as ordure picked up by a shoe) reduce memory to decoration, unaccountable artifact
as bodies float in a Winogrand photograph, propelled by trampoline, French owner hurling
his dog across the canal into Duchamp's lap. My Kai-yu Hsu, bound in Singapore, has on
    its cover
reversed characters and a red seal, no longer classic,
                on the chemistry table
                a marmoset

The Woman of Wax

is recollection of petal, fine cheek scratched through blush, so much carved mastodon
    seamed by years's implication
as pharaoh's boat warped to unusability, ribs deforming out of pins, deck planks scrap
in a trench with flax rope a royal barge. You pass shadows of people with wolf beaks,
dogs which object to your smell, forgetting the tusk was wedged in beefy jaw
(as Buckles Woodcock's wife impaled by one) a gesture toward the fixed, imagine
since this is made of this it will be lasting, prospective as a ripening tomato,
grape's must glaze, the horn heard in The Dark Hills, a hearkiness of impetus
as when the sacred text boxed exudes enclosednesslichkeit, aroma of the
possibility of flavor. The flower vase is urn for us, our hearts peeled
like mangoes or radishes for display, enshrined gazable, Hoc est corpus poffle,
barebreasted one's spiky crown so like a medieval queen's, angevin nose
and snakes around the arm like rolled clay bracelets done in spirals, offers us
the gift of decoration, ritual Jane Harrison could imagine. It's not our business
not our fault that other religions existed or crept happily to cult as kitten with yarn,
stepped-on slug brought in as a gift, our flowerlike, beelike insides not "spilled"
out but, like everything, displayed. An inch above our skin we feel angles and edges
intend our division, the snake a binding for arms withering in place.

Louis Dixhuitieme Son Histoire

could be anything at all, George's sword (Cappadocian) and dragon
armorial as patchiest ignorance of French, rosiest rose windows
in Henry Adams's so-to-be-visited Chartres, absorbing to its name
Proust's church on the pré, Yeats's Notre Dame in Pound's vignette,
anything unerased in *Paul et Virginie* engravings, and the street,
described in the Boston subway, enameled on steel, where the printers

used to throw their old type, pigs rootling notch-edged types, barefoot
newsboys raised on *Pluck and Luck* and Dickens's history of England
reset in thready Cary from copies brought from England as Irish
four-volume quarto Blackstone *Commentaries* replicated double folio
at half the price, a pocket Pindar less likely to be reproduced than Horace
(always, they say, in Jefferson's pocket, his Monticello first with a dome
over a lemon room they found no use for that should've been atelier),
as that century feeds into the nineteenth retaining these shreds, as Nichol Smith
says Thomson's *Seasons* is in origin the Scottish border, and it's
been a while no longer hip to say with Perry and others Gray's precursive
of Romance in its romantic aspect. These things through finest
smoke of steel engraving are invariably French as if a portrait of Jusserand
appears before his book on journeys, Quixote's Palmerin there like
the platy dragon in Saint George still somehow rose, not greeny as in
Grunewald or the Johnson portrait never meant bound I found loose
in Dublin, engraved facing (under the oval) bricks, localia tinting old rags.

Itself Defined

"I not unnaturally came to think of these facts as common
property." Jacques Barzun, somewhere or other

I saw an eggshaped stainless continental coffeemaker, organic as this peppershaker showing
Saxifrage oppositifolia, fivepetaled it seems, the usual fat roseleaf shape, coming to points
(the salt is borage, set before real ivy in wicker, unnoticed because not porcelain) and so
we see the unpredictability of what constitutes a set, perhaps why mammy he and she
Quatrale pepper say they both, because spice, are one, variant on the frog or duck rainboots
ineluctably left and right, subject for Yeats, fit because few, the limited set, our preference
in aliens for three sexes, geometrically ribald. A life of courses in the common life, that in
        which
we're asleep, fits you to think there's them, l'altri tapable on the refrigerator with widepoled
        magnets
flat as wafers (themselves like salt and pepper, north and south, shapes) and privitous us,
        subject of
this and that but subject, incarnate theme, the labeling of a thing's fat content, resoluble ash
ancestral coming out of the borage hole, speckling to our startlement the morning egg
what's to say beyond "oh yes, we owe ourselves, it to ourselves, congenial grit,
because in our understandings progenitive," displacement of the singular, emanative,
        pocketed, preserved,
the Duchess of Malfy proclaimed by her mole Sophonisba, or Marlowe's (The New of
        Malta in a mislettered
binding I should have bought in Pangloss), crashing through the floor to the oilpot
a function of novelty, or perhaps the definition.

Another Weeping Virgin

In Blanco, Texas exudes myrrh (their supposition is) caught in cotton swabs
fit to anoint the feet of small minorities for photographs. I think of Francis Bacon
for whom a garden was a little Eden, who first imagined *and* conceived science as
separate from philosophy not so long ago, mistress Ceres his master, the rhetoric euphuist
      antitheses,
our balance our beginning, not how much it weighs but what weights match
and what would the dear modern in his beaver hat say to an icon's doxic runnels
so much what one had come in Geneva to expect, unabsolvable bushels of shards
so close to what had been Bishop Jewel's pet hate's reprinted claybrown boards
like lips so prim compressed. I'd like a miracle less flashy to the common mind, a shift
in the spectrum bands of strontium, our bishop too willing to say for what "she" cries,
mouthpiece for painted glands. The newspaper's screened one feels moist. He says
reproductions do, or might do, what this one does, that it's bad magic to move it
from the house trailer to the new basilica. That we do agree any knotted rag's a doll
named Dulcie gives you nothing, no ground dear bishop to address us, believers,
as willing to put that weight on she she doesn't (weeping) ask. You're a bandit of the cloth
as much as any radio bible geek, afraid the superstition of your own constituents
will melt all if it melts. Swab on your own cheeks as miracle what her must emits.
The icon's in heat. Asphaltum as a tinting glaze contains tar which collects in points
in hot weather bleeding right through varnish, Sir Joshua Reynolds's faces fallen
from that cause. Say Bing Crosby in a stylish parish suit
brings up the point, beards the madonna then says but ah, who's not to say
the virgin's ruined channels aren't genuine, marvelous though explicable
and sings. There is that is to say once you admit the pronoun she
no limit to vulgarity and this *is* if you like a point of grammar, the
history of weeping itself (I wrote) not imposture. "Five pellets Sunday night," Haining
wrote under the heading *Turtles,* "Can on their home in Morgan's room," and this though
      his phrasing isn't verse
because he knew we'd catch the "their" even before "home," no question of veracity as
      today in Goodwill
I saw a typed hornbook text on a wood paddle, under plastic laminate with upholsterer's
      tacks.

Scotch Economists

The without with which we do's so little ours, we think, reprehensible in terms of recht
to want beyond our sphere, "the inside and the outside are the same" and my baby needing
      bread
would make biology a limit, protoscorpion's book lungs emancipating its aquatic forebear,
      refinement
of gill, Gurth's metal collar raw material, umbrellas at the funeral vestigial prayerbook.
Organismic thocht's ae given to surprised reduction, the stairs in a black and white film
I saw very young which at the touch of a lever collapse like louvers, skulking malignity visible
through eyeholes in pictures. I resolved the terror by making heavy cardboard portraits with
ingeniously pivoted ovals behind to be eyes like the odd ones from a pistol trigger or butterfly
hinge in the Boston science museum purportedly transmuting one kind of motion to another.
      The dog's
archetypal stick chewed becomes unarchetypal bits. Desire is a holding together of that

which lacks a causal nexus, indescribable as the photograph of child on swing in David's
  mental
experiment beginning to move, pendular haze not mentioned by Bergson as a kind of comedy.
Our lives do without the possessive, owning nothing (given no clothing) and banks preserve
  us sticks and leaves,
saying it's illusion a trick the disenfranchised burning ricks, breaking frames down to sticks
employ eliminating means to gain ends, a short while political economy imagined or
  pretended to
imagine nations as cobblers with adjacent shops (now ranch homes each are nations) in
  spite of which
need is not a network, *i.e.,* reciprocal as physics's amp's potentially a kind of photon and
  it's again
grotesque for labor billboards in Detroit saying keep assembly local, vivid as the facts are,
  to think them facts, aquaria
in the California earthquake (we're told), losing water up from the tank, en bloc, rectilinear
as if a motion bass enough would translate without changing, imagination the integument
  around a concept,
"variable" swimming in its skin through Stewart, Reid, Mackintosh, Valéry, minds
  invariantly fluid.
Yet those gifted at it, Adam Smith, Mill, Lamb on his East India House cratchit stool
imagined bales and barrels as part of a language as Spinozans distinguish
implicit structure from teaching mode, silks wrapped around china. In fact it's better if
the packing material's disposable, available at-site, not every advance's manifold a
  shippable whole.

Natural Allusions

The stubble over the grave is made of paper, five or six times thicker
than blades of grass. The grave markers could be anything, balsa, celastic
and this is sufficient, the fainting sofa in the room a set, not floating
in the pool. (Some lilypads will stand up flat and sideways.) No matter, that water
may have stones with flattish surfaces clear of water, floating *for* feet, and
waterfalls led into irregular channels may nourish ferns. Any degree of artificiality,
clear marbles for pebbles, thick in a stream bed, the new age jeweler's habit of
putting a little pewter pegasus or something hopelessly fey in a halved geode, making
it a fortunately found, but found, grotto, as if an old boot might have children in it
or the sheep in a Connecticut field painted by Innes bleat, extra touch brutalizing something
into shape. Some one thing dressed dresses everything, Francis Bacon's keepers
keep Bacon from ruining his finished paintings but are they privileged
to tell him when he's done? angels in Giotto (I suppose there are)
are less flashy than Tiepolos, aware of how light hits angels. Rembrandt
fingers the feathers. Savarin tells stories about gourmands lying back groaning after meals
in expiation, experience denied Pascal, and those cherubs in saintly Boucher pictures
function as sheep, pastorality beyond care, displayed naked in a river, the sheep
"just out of the picture." Saying it, less than generic, has edges, we
give them to it as New Orleans people make themselves costumes, in
unaffordable lamé a year's fruition, to walk beside as if shepherding
(or seconding) some float, rich by ascription as a church, the anything of it,
grass flowing over terrain like some slime mould or frown on a bulldog brow, Orson Welles
  as Churchill.

The bishop in analogy a notched carrot. We've had enough of de Chirico
space as space, Bridge of Sighs's floor tile, when it's really the metal bands
you forced the naked man in, sitting on him like a suitcase, thighs against ribs
an hour or so, blood from the orifices not exceptional as if doctrine were something to crack
    like a pecan
or flea that otherwise would leap or roll away, our running dog repeating rabbit rainbow dew.

Artists' Studios

Listening to David Anderson talk about giant tables, small very thick "turbine"
pieces, best mock-French oriental painter's box—oval with cylinders at each side
with dots and dashes, footed steel swordguard for a Japanese bank president's office,
    perfect flat
one with two slots, Sung, Tang and a fine Li Po bar sign, neon behind simplified cutouts
with tassels (bubblewrapped for shipping), "Now, the cylinders have moved outdoors, too"
like infinitely deep characters in helvetica. Bored with most vases (except the one
on the steel table going to an Italian restaurant in Hong Kong), giant Mai Tais
with parasols (drools of chain over lip, really hung from a peg like pasta).
Sam Scott's *rincon,* saying the ground color outside is raw sienna, "This is the Southwest,"
his anecdote about shaman dancers like his painting, and violent firefly pastels on black
a neptune symbol below accidental, meant as a plant, this notion that you can push through to,
in paint. "The artist's responsibility is to lead," revised in afterthought to "call attention,"
not liking them, my eyes going, crossed-through scribbles "like" his paint in no interesting
    respect,
his one big long one called BEYOND WORDS half erased, Rimbaud, Laforgue, "a diamond
    light," he says.
Now writing this *on* Eugene Newmann's stages-of-a-painting flyer enclosing cercopithecines
in pencil on wretched paper ripped (before we came) off a sheet with more monkeys on his
    door
so we've just heads and in the middle an upthrust from a prehensile tail mostly below the
    tear,
thank you Eugene. Then Doris Cross's Quaker Oats cylinders in her kitchen, spare
words pared to letters and benignant face, we find what she'd do with ZERO to ZOUAVE,
    last page
of Merriam Webster and "New Mexico Essayed" (Don't . . . tease me), kinds of knots in
    KNOWLEDGE
and Jerry West's slides of bulls, the billboard, in the room awake with dying Dad,
tin chimneyed nuclear cellar, canned fetuses in jars, bandolier corn god's cornfield in
New Mexico, hand grenades, "The Search," two men lumpish in bear suits with lantern
truffing through foreground like winter Remingtons, and the kid on
stilts over Pet Milk cans, a miniature town with on the middle hill marbles.
We've a Hopi teacup they say's thirties touristware, thick in raw umber and blackfigure
    pattern.
Doris with Guston catalogue for the show she went to New York to see, twitting me on
    "monosyllabism" she'd,
by tactical excision, float first, blow up (she said) Zeus and set him beside his column of Z's,
West's fish bearing the naked lovers, barely (he says) hanging on, reflection in its eyes, red
    threads in gills
John Connell's tarsoaked rat with questing mouth bang on in Carol's hands

comes back like the ashtrays Maria, legendary potter made, a polaroid Morning Star made
of a shaman (maybe) headdress like a judge's wig, ermine with horns attached by beads to
    crown
and a walrusheaded marlin flattening to pierced paperknife they say's a wound plug insertable
in animal, dyed porcupine on cups, a peregrine falcon amulet in redorange pipestone
everything around here doubly patinated, adobado as paint around organpipely secular
    Quakers, Vermeer's back to us in Newmann's latest reduction radiant blot.

Science Project

I built a bowl of breakfast food, grape-nuts and all-bran (the kind like sticks)
then nutri-grain wheat, heaping, soaked it in milk then pressed down the wheat flakes,
let it sit. Cut into it's a bank, the sort Dürer or Ruskin might choose to paint,
first stones, then sticks, then leafy mould, top layer so cohesive it overhangs
oh demonstration in a white bowl that Eberhart was right to get off
on a decomposing groundhog, so like a charcoal fire in a brazier, kind of thing Ficino used
with a pierced cover to throw constellations on his vaulted ceiling (keyed in its colors
to earth, sky, the ocean's silver, basically an Aurignacian cave with scope,
richest materials provided by those who'd learned to mine, to weave), something eastern
in his sensibility as if he thought the Greeks spoke Arabic. Odd to think of
a language as, in itself, subversive, having to compare it to Florentine illiterates
going mad for St. Pragma's thumb, that you'd think Savonarola a remark
about religious grammar, what mattered as much as their elf shoes noodling to points (see
the History of Woodcut) not what their food was but what it looked like on the plate,
ptarmigan, bit of barley, carrot like Hans Hofmann's Long Island house, each angle
and visual drop a danger, Leonardo's bluegreen background landscapes really food,
or garden as in Boston a smart shop paid a man to sculpt its sand with a bit of plaster
to hills like Utah, Idaho and the fun was watching him stand in the gulleys with a hose
sprinkling them to geological remarks, anecdotal and boring as the fishermen on bridges
in my Scottish grandmother's blue willow ware on which she served beef roast,
salmon, wheat toast with jugged plum jam full of the shreds of skin stiff, folding to needles
    sharp as pine.

Fireplace Poodles

What's (Cavell in *Artspace*) a proper subject for philosophy, profound question you might
    revise
to what is the difference between a proper subject for philosophy and ditto for art, since
photographers now exhibit roomsful of "European staircases," Virgil saying my theme is
    Theme,
imaginable translated by Dryden to rhyme neat as a sewing basket or stylized drawing
of Thanksgiving turkey, the rhymes drumsticks . . . philosophers *address* questions,
    Descartes
muddling through "substance" imagining wax. You could have Giger design for Jimenez
    to cast reptilian innards
to house the Dallas Museum of Art, entrance device purely psychological, to lead you to it,

funneling in of mood. It shouldn't matter what a museum has in—anything, your kitchen chair

(certainly mine, spray-painted black over black to repair the damage done by rubber-base enamel,

the bentwood chairs Flora Searcy gave me when I was poor in Dallas ditto, from their green and yellow pea

to catch us up to deco), our Hopi teacup on a bookcase in the living room as if for reference.

It's magical to turn and see things, then away, send curators piñon incense to remind them of Santa Fe

wholly unable to understand folds in earth driven through, flown over, as if you shut your eyes and what you dream of

you think about, the subject (cantly) choosing you. Anderson's export tea caddies like three-leaf clovers translated up leaving a plasma trail, lobate body in pewter suggests a shape

to a sculptor's already a subject, exploited in the act of recognizing it as a subject,

following the fourteen-year-old girl home, rattling candy (why not a Prince Albert can?) so make

a flower more durable than a vase, welded washers to be petals on a spitty coathanger, draw

on the vase scenes: Socrates delaying a second in the agora, watching puppets, Charles Dickens

in a club being drawn unawares by Thackeray, a naked Priapus seeing a swatch of blossom

for the first time as bronze sculpture. There's no way for philosophy to leave room for gentility,

diner filled with Segal customers, when it's the sound of dime on formica, shoved under plate

the frequency of it meaningless as rain but still a recurrent index of materials, measure of surfaces

one milled on the thin edge, the other incorporating what seem real gold flecks.

Blueprint Facades

Tilly fally said Johnson, dismissing nonsense, paint in squishy crosses in middle Guston giving way

to KKK discoursers, painters with pillowcase heads like Ackerman's Ling, mailart nonentity who, hooded,

drinks red wine through the cloth, nose visible through his single eyehole, string of wet paintings of

(so early) boots, lightbulb with chain enlarged to squashy individual rounds, illegal gunmen in a car with slats

as if any nail half hammered into wood is typical of the failed event of painting a picture, thwarted intent

for no reason, as if we've all been wrong to paint anything beyond the hideous banal, like the

perception that falling dust is audible (his wristwatch with one hand, enough to signify) and it is cruel,

living in a world of knees, his poems called *Pink Buildings,* stuffed chair over nearly obliterated them.

David says it's a window behind it; the proofs for and against it would be interesting, no pots in corners

as Jimenez's spike cacti get so decorative on his *Pieta* they wouldn't let him hang so to speak in

the Old Town park, disappointingly cartoon, not so good as oleo originals (probably because you know that

hideous painting had somewhere an original, so this *is* David's posited first Sleeping
    Mexican in donkey cart
erected by the city fathers but after the fact, at the end of a run as Krazy Kat and Francis
    Bacon's pendant bulbs
are flotsam in Guston lithographs of bulbs and bedsteads, shoes, the nail in the wall a hook,
    enough nailheads
slightly elongate a park, and you wish he'd have done (over) that damned church O'Keeffe
    couldn't keep
hands off, the so elegant buttress like slab clay propping slab (say Dylan Thomas leaning
    against Henry Treece)
and there are mental experiments. Look at any figurative painting as if it's an aquarium
    full of
water either occupied by or the figures painted on the back wall of, it. A German says
    there's no genuine
possibility of motion in antique art though Hittite soldiers alive and dead *in* the waves seem
instantiations of a kind of counterproof, the odd king here and there who really wanted dance
on his wall, in his *presence* (Treece says) blinded to the cocky strut, and some patrons
    would want
without knowing it presence of that kind, the moment of spear into lion, tremor along the
    lance,
"grate against ribcage" Pound would say nostalgic for some classical measure as if
    weeping would solve it
Guston on the contrary fixed in the moment's jello fixity, all there is all there is
as if Stevens sunning himself naked on a Jamaica beach were to say almost anything at all.
Outside my window a bush with a hollow in it in which a sparrow has been. You make the
bush a brain or a bush. Paint, he says, doesn't make anything anything.   •

Wimsey's Degree

The atlas-eater with a jaw for newts wouldn't like at all my dead toad in a
peanutbutter jar with foodstore alcohol over, wide leaf still clinging to the belly, so
new dead the eyes are still distinguishable jelly, Clio found walking
the dog, its twisted-on cap in spite of initial testing now leaking a little,
wrapped in a napkin inside a zip-lock baggie, time enough to see
it as fate, Anatomie splayed in astringent and absorptive medium, short feet the
flippers of all our guilt, sign that analytic intelligence outruns cruelty, kind to be petty
this toad now swollen some as we intended from negative osmosis and delightful habit
of alcohol molecules collapsing into water how can we, ignorant of taxonomy
expect this flottant spectacle (black draymen in Whitman, shirtless, the same) to
be other than Thomas Gray, the exhibition of sensitivity, delectation as Chas Dee Mitchell
    says
in glint of crystal left in morning Chatterton's phial, maker of jellied eye
(but not as in Beddoes who'd prefer the hollow) a lyric intuition, reason
for chastity or some other esoteric virtue, the time amiss
for wrongs to gender picturesque virtues. Take on the police-court subject, point to toad
deceased before coroner's convened, this winged man with roundy buttocks floating
like Leonard Baskin's birthday invitation under a round red moon the
sign that trousered decency deserves its zinc, so scratched and folded
as any beercan multiply run over sunk into asphalt becomes, innocent of print,

a blazon or shield's blazon for us, that which, looked at in morning light or sulfur evening produced

Icarean confidence in the flying man, armless in Gaza, over Somerville's

gas-station vista of lumber shops and truckable paper plates compact,

the suburb Lucifer sold a braying Irish faust, great parking lot for his daughter's wedding reception's vacancy,

ignored as Coursey says even visually-minded friends listing what's

in the field of view ignore massive vaned and cabled electrical stations gray to be invisible, the hurricane fence around private pool, hot tub's cedar elevation, those simmering in clouds of vapor invisible to neighbor delectation as business-suited people flying like herons past the moon or flipbook Citgo shield in Boston, Lovecraft's notion that the toadlike beings owning Ipswich, known by difficulty as, belong to Dagon as middle management evolves suspenders framing of its floral ties too bright for toppered overseers the Yard a place these others go to play at, quit of all but tactic duty.

Plate Print

No, it's wrong to think of it as whip or spine diagram, any more than mother and child is Madon-na

and its complexities of rhetoric like heat-sensitive pits, viprous, his Eve a shaved rabbit. Firstly Eve

was more formidable, the Garden her métier, she knowing classifications, reasons why there should be

no such thing as snake, as Darwin on his gravel walk at Down, with spaniel, noticed nearly everything

as functive factors, worm-casts at sides of paths suggesting they avoid a hesitant tread

repeated, plug hat on bald head, scarf dark as anything in Gorey, coat dark as Welles's in *The Third Man,*

will have seen snakes, knowing what the chances are. So she, hearing this Lyle's syrup voice from leaves

(quick now, here now, &c.) knew from the hiss and body's S, embodied script, that he was French,

had little poems about graveyards by the sea before there were graves, in short was a guest

as such blessed, béate, integument the color of Chinese tattooing given a metallic element.

We marvel he is cool, and she naked and *pale,* possessed of the nape they thought admirable the hair up, la!

and violet tints in it held her end up to imaginings of persuasion. It doesn't matter that the snake

we see is extended in a figure, thing you'd shake dashing droplets, rite's prop, because in Eden

shiny rather than salt glazes covered the same clay, our white parents bauxitish in their oxide ash,

not flushed and various as roadside mangos but the same white as outcropped rock, any painted-on reflections were,

as leaves and grass greenglazed with yellow under made a statement, did for sky so we'd not

imagine birds and that which Milton thought spoke Hebrew sharing air. The myth's no myth we can use

except for decorators, the scene a gaudy buckle, prosodic showcase. You need simplicity, as in liking a ballon rouge for its own sake to take it all as reference, rather than allusion. When you do the rattler shrinks (as he so

wisely observed) to toad because the creature from its point of view's a wall, solid as if the word quest

might be, this once, redeemed and Keats correct to make his watercolor, pleasure paleness rather than Japanese

beetle's underblush in green and gold sheathed wings, their curve nearly defined by fractive modulation.

Reprise

Fix her into the ground like a corn spindle, you could start it off, thinking as Eshleman says

stone Venuses were found that way, compromised by observers, their pumice-like surfaces pushed in

fine earth, drying mud like lightbulbs or amphorae inexplicably pointed, spindled attention, gatepost planting,

see as significant the filling of beach hole with water (Creeley's poems to holes) or alamos

dissolved to beach, what little Swinburne or Tennyson's children might have done on the Isle of Wight

yet more impressive to shape a stone as if for animal, the mind imagining plane as flank as we used

to genuflect toward (guided toward) dim candle in red glass. Bury a toad, singular fancy to bury a toad,

invited by roadside signs to caves, living limestone added to by ground flood and rain drip,

difficult passages cemented over, railings thin for the hand, clammy pipe give, allow, permit rust its season also

there being a wish to do (and do) a'thing, take up a fallen bit of limestone and dig it, upended,

in mirror-flat river sand, as Banks said footprints left one year are there the next, or habit of naming the formations, asking

children if they can see Santa Claus or bat, poached eggs, pancakes invasion from the Black Forest notion

that habitations are edible, that the components are, this toad (about the size of a pebble goddess) from its

own wee cave, cavity pluckt by hunger, felled by what the insects ate, ecosystem foundered on tree roach control

to no greatly available purpose, slight whitening of belly in spite of alcohol, time to go back to

the ground, enjarred, infinitive fence a habit of thinking of the noun attended by hooded verbs

their dirge pregrammatical, issuing from no particular source, as music on Prospero's island

or a slight touch of dankness in vaguest scent of alcohol escaping from container's lid

tells you from, lid, escaping, toadlike ester issuant from what's buried by deposition gives us

any range of ritual utterance readymade to fill the air, sceptered Neptune's unicorn on publisher's seal

a formality, as Texans talk of "putting up" a thing, shelves always above eye level folded into jelly jar

meniscus, wave flattening to beach in which stray fruit is stoppered goddesses.

Insinuating Marx

Here is a copybook Marx ("for beginners") with a funny drawing of him, bound in calendered
cream paper tinted to look like kraft brown bag. He is winking. The appearance
of ease suggests, more geometricum guarantees from its simplified nature (eyebrows
reduced to fins on cars, no iron in that frame) picture of how we wished to imagine having
    come at learning.
Edward Batchelder imagining his office wanted dimestore frames with the original photos,
    generic relatives and why not,
Marta, Baby Jason, dog; it's hard to say what this would be a remark about but the good
    postcard photo
of Marx looking like Twain and Poe, Conrad bearded, Justice as Edward VII puts us in a
    posture of admiring
to which, like Shaw, he won't have been indifferent. Those who make their mark mark
    their mark.
LOVE GOD. WORK FOR FOOD. CARL REEVES a cardboard sign he holds,
    cleanshaven, a very firm chin
and I've no work for him except putting himself in my poem, "Let's check that against the
    profit made from a worker's labour,"
expensively cheapened like the cover of this Pantheon comic. The post office sells a
    Stampin' game for Christmas,
longlashed moppets collecting four of a kind, the stamp's decorative function (say appeal)
    separate from its function
as proof. Haining's engraved ones, Poe and so on, These Immortal Chaplains (sunk)
    lace-edged from ripping along
imagined perforations, glued on his magazine's stamp page to be . . . play, something
    complicated an appeal, like
ordinary food arranged well. Adam Smith's world proved itself to him; imagine him asking
    a class
of mobile farmlads living in college on their sack of meal, what would be required to
    enshrine Marx's portrait
on a US stamp (I know there weren't strictly stamps till I suppose G. B. Hill and the penny
    post, the prepaid
wafer taking gradually over, motile frank), the Monte dei Paschi invitation on marvelous
    Italian paper still I suppose in Maud's hands
like that in feel with its triple hills impressed in rag in letterpress. Think long enough about
    units and you'll write in them
Mickey Mouse on the cover of a twenty-nine-cent notepad not as I first thought reduced by
    digital means to squares
but really a mosaic or design for one, cleanshaven mouth smirking like Carol's under
    Indonesian print. Cassell lost
Stevenson's original *Treasure Island* map, "harbours that pleased me like sonnets:" he
    had another drawn, ten years of mine
mislaid (it seems, permanently) at Little, Brown (workingman with wrench and cap facing
    Uncle Sam with dog evenly matched
enough, both ink) and if our cars were Cuernavacan we firstly wouldn't own them, then
    they'd be these
tapioca pastels as if the car *were* separate from your sorbet house, Mickey's skin altering
    with climate,
Chilean Chesterton on handlettered page 111's promised "we communists will rally to the
    cause of the workers," most moving a

facsimile Erasmus (in all these pickup drawings) crosshatched "by the Spanish Inquisitors
because he was a 'heretic' "
vulnerable in the plane of all the other drawings, funny lecturers dismissing Aquinas as
wordy fool.

Emblems

Or parts for wholes, the folkorists looking at a shee-na-gig in stone (lovingly reproduced,
all the porosity in place, effect of drawn seals perfect and monumental, Acropoline in
Themis)
getting infinite value out of the mouth expression, some slot or wholly ambiguous cavity,
like the
straight line in Have A Day buttons, any round textured thing gone to line and stipple, then
described, as antiquarians inferred personality from Roman coins, multiple portraits of one
emperor, ranged in a plush drawer. Give us Marcus Aurelius, gowk looking younger than
we thought,
mouth uncertainly stern, true melting Stoic, this image pressed in clay then cast in wax
for the artisan to render in a line cut as Germany used to issue folios of endless tomb
inscriptions awesomely musty
unlike for charm Jones's Stonehenge plates, peeringly irregular in Piranesi light or
Hydriotaphia
pots looking always southwest's jagged yet feathery stripes, these promises,
pre-photograph, that
line cuts of effigies repay attention. It's a convention looking at them that we see or will
the interpretation laid on by the author who so lovingly broke the text to supply us with
as on a beach you, coming on a ring of stones and charcoal drowned in sand feel obliged
to date, add the time element, Ortega's patch of faded blue proclaiming its antiquity
on its face.

Ms. Cross and the Angel

Doris, given a renaissance St. Michael promptly disregarded the face, knew the
hands (folded like salad tossers) had to be saved, saw a third of the face and throat
an animal nose, not hopelessly angelic, touch of embroidery below the crew neck a dribbling
mouth,
more fleur de lis-ish ornament on the dark gown as little dancing men, perhaps
winged, perhaps more like sunflowers but certainly dancing. Asked if Hofmann were
a gentleman she looked dumbfounded, said after a long pause he was *probably* a gentleman
but this painter, an Italian with a name like Little Loaf, had he seen her thumbs
blank out his halo, dismiss the gilded membrane wings, remark "she's had
at least two miscarriages," and this was more than anecdotal because so very much an
instance
of seeing a thing freshly, not thinking you *can* see it, can see. Last night we glommed
illuminarios, paper bags with candles in lines on the ground, on walls, on roofs, some with
the kraft seams random, a few alternate or nearly, tops turned down like regency boots
(Jorrocks

still shown with them, inside of the calf pale tan they now sell as armbands, decoration
I suppose like this angel's wings or face, conventional piety over infinitely
nonferal hands was brute, an ogre of a thing appliquéd all over
with floral flying Munchkin men.

Burnt Horses

Tissot did a picture of London tourists, peering about, two Christ's hospitaliers in their
long blue coats and—surprising—knee breeches, long stockings, impossible
not to think of Charles Lamb, ex-Hospitaler much later in his life
affecting the same in black and wrote so well of Jem White's sweeps, given
sausage annually, as a Victorian painter later juxtaposed streetgirl with flowers
and even younger crossing-sweeper, male, intriguing (perhaps) Dickens
that stance we have of objectless compassion not usually evoked by barefoot
cleanly lads in country France, pale gypsies there for stunted tree trunk, adoze by russet
     cow, the
paraphernalia of poverty, how do those rags close there (what button or thong)?
so like in a way watching the excavation at Knight, was it, in Dallas
shadowed in side light, huge for a building now up, in which for the first
time I saw the illusion of liquid—not water, not air, either maybe, *fill* an empty
excavation, dwarfed cementmixing trucks's tilted bottles collaborating with shadow but
immersed in ideal fluid, somehow separated from rough chalk walls defining edges, incline
     road
defining depth, an emotion from one not really like pretending the toy theater fairy palace's
wrecked ships and chests, Poseidon's Attic, nereid are there for us in air we can imagine
lit by gas, this placing *ourselves* in space supposititious as if Norton's garden's cloud-made
     brim
kept flat by surface tension might have on it if we imagine them ghostly lilies
floating like the word hibiscus you might almost, reaching, pick, the spirit a
dytiscus as Yeats (throwing out) MacDiarmid saved, description of the febrile thrill
needing to be filled out, even *for* its effect, a touch of science, budbreasted nymph's Icarian
lyre tuned to some presumptive intervals, if not at least thick strings for deeper notes.

Fair Copies

the photo of Jane Burden in a posture Rossetti adopts, Bobby Ross's Beardsley memoir
     with medallion-
clean vignettes, drawings he'd do over so quickly when suppressed, John Bull's pizzle
     tiny as an
epicanthic fold, women's hair being dressed while everyone is naked, so much more
     interesting
than ape carmen though Sacheverel's on English artisans tempts me to his sister's *Bath.* The
antinomy is this: the bright originals (Doris doesn't believe there are originals) don't add much
after all to what twists to a shape inside a frame or *part* of body done in clay and cast.
Perhaps the pieces of paper that made curlers were pinned in place. Tiny model
offices from India show white superiors' white kepis on the desk top left above the inkpot
turbaned help below each with a tilted desk's paper's script like Arabic, scrawled business.

What's this to me and of course the curl-papers were pinned. Music in a picture
is not meant to be played or read though Ruskin suggests you paint the effect
of a complicated paisley. I'm told the film with black miners underground lit by bulbs
is darkest yet, as Beardsley'd invent ways for black to creep over Wagnerites (evening
    dress) or masquerades
(night is a mask) or those flowers every whichway on a black gown to show you where folds
you can't see go, though always complete. A bald head and a large hat equivalent dish.
I've added rubber glue to today's penholders which otherwise'd eat the points. A woman
in the Indian museum showed us mosaic and lace turquoise in silver but we prefer a heavier
bracelet with larger rounds separated by loops, not fat but substantial, of silver
at right angles to its longest curve, like epaulets in Oz or drawn lines of force around the
    wire's axis.

The Pattern of Repentance

Grass nearly gray as white buildings on a gray day supports in a giant square
whitetail deer, fat rabbits, birds nearly exotic as the cockatiel made by distance gray
or thinlined as the half domestic turkey blend, clock in the square almost carillon tower
tolling clunk, no reason to describe the bleak light gray become light purple,
Hartford in a purple light. Living rough as Peary at the pole, dried corn in polyethylene.
There are squares like this in Dublin, any country given to Palladian gray stone, the
effect of any neutral color as horizon on a long square, multiple of squares, a column in
or near the center, paving somehow lost to scale as if wheat or something not our business
    to distinguish.
A bleakness not like what is laid on you in gothic, not of time stopped but going on as a
postage stamp slips under the thumb, significance of the passage its indefiniteness. One
    thinks
of our plains sprinkled with buffalo, same slippage of "our," the animals in their giant square
having eaten all the corn, though any in particular if approached is too full for it,
engravings of such squares that put in carriages, equipage, period occupants less to us
    than the plan
that in its rectitude could be a duplicate of this, shadows of Europe
whipping like Fellini gossamer, no matter, the deer ahistorical, preceding tainted mite.

Rude Shocks

abrupter things, corner on a comma, lean toward
the twenties rhyme (or off-rhyme—tennis with golf)
that means you own it all, *mentally* uneasy with none
of it because, confronted with vicar, tea sandwiches, long aunts
able to name them. Unfranchised detectives watch silver wedding
presents for which there are no names, a sense as of
something omitted by simple neglect (Chesterton's postman or filcher
of apostle spoons) and here in this fat *Temblor* I'm
named, as a species, whelk turning to make lateral or cross-marked
blotches on a shell, records of mantle. You take a
trip to the country of the Georgics, find lead whitening

under dung, cyder crossing ferment plateaux in the barrel,
and the dog's new pee gleams like tinsel on the
morning grass. It doesn't matter after a while what
country houses and Iceland offer as subjects; it's
whether new lines begin with and or the
or something meatier that, like season tells
Diggon we're ready for lambing, time for
charges' birth, one's social status like fleece.
Not that it was easy, rhyming come with dream, but that one supposedly
had time for rhyming contests and being smitten
in that state yet knew the practicalia, dangers attendant
on the ewe on which as Heinzelman points out the comer,
prepared to lecture, turned into something complicated as a
secondclass ticket holding one's place in a Nicholas Blake
found, shall we say, between the pages seventy-seven and seventy-eight, record
for the mind only of whitsun platforms, verse the equivalent
of discarded sport equipment, our pastoral wrapped sandwich,
Froy in the baggage car a labeled tea.

Kata

and other forms of karate, things calling themselves kwon do, and we find
a fighting sequence is a thing to learn, each a kata
and the pigtailed young things look like ballet but the older ones
scream, presenting themselves like battered ashcans, graceful Mehitabels, the
rule, so quick to strike, feint or quiver in place, and it helps for
some of the rabid parents' children to acquire a foul or two, a broken rule
discomfiting the sons of gentlemen. The women look as if concepts of fairness are foreign,
properly abandoned. The potential opponent pulling a blow inches from the judge
may not make points. Reaching out from chest pain let it be known . . . squirrels
fall out of trees. Some of them live. Arboreal monkeys exhibit fractures, dissected.
Think of Bertrand Russell passing through California, doing a little teaching
and me who never broke a bone in this hangar with ten areas laid out in tape,
yellow as some of the more initial belts. It's nothing to see minorities threaten air with
    billhooks
but the sons and daughters of middle Middyl, bowing to experts, the bareness
of infinite feet leads us as if by a twisted finger to think of the homes, many
it seems with videocams, how normal they must be without quilted or felt
tops (some with US flags as arm patches, some trousers made of bunting) and here
in a form too pure what to do with one's formidability, Lawrence's gold
buying bedou, H. F. Heard's honeyseeking missiles
even a kind of cross-dressing by country, ours later genuinely invisible
in black socks cloven for the sandal, hooded ninja. Dick
Woodworth, over six feet tall, went to Japan to study Aikido,
do it properly and met, coming out of the hills, one master
inimitably brutal, making nonsense of its innocence, but leaving
no opponent, however tall, able to rise for the parting bow. Applaud him.

Mode d'Emploi

Today a man on the street near a baby-blue laundry basket, some clothes strewn around
adjusting, endlessly adjusting dark blue shorts voluminous as bloomers
reaching down inside, pulling up the waist, rolling the hems to thick tubes
otherwise naked, pale, say middleweight, looking down with that
preoccupation of the derelict given to possessions as if care for Goodwill castoffs is place,
occupation, the French reflexive, I occupy myself with things, things occupy me
the young policeman in dark blue short sleeves "Are you okay?" or something,
audible across several lanes, the man like a jogger till I passed
a low stone coping by the college's employment office, lovely building
near the stadium where having signed as a temp, conscious of occupation
thought it not unnatural, a man adjusting his jock strap, settling running shorts
till as is the way persistence of activity as in Osbert Sitwell's palsy, the tiny steps
that if not curbed would take him into traffic through the pigeons tipped
me it's what cats and dogs do thwarted in an action, the witless grooming
perfectly acceptable but unprepared for, lacking margin or foyer, our
actions guaranteed by slither of begin, drip of aftermath.
For us the odd sock in the dryer, squareholed coinage, that which used
(that which we are used to do, Burke would've said) is all our usability
small clothes still in a sense in the basket, the basket itself clothing.

Gents at Holyhead

A head, it seems, for C. Day Lewis appearing in a melting snowman
or basiled in a statue's head, fallen from a tree the sudden eruption of that pale, white,
    unwanted
was an image he might have given Clark Lectures on and maybe does, in a heaven reserved
    for thirties intellectuals
who built enough of them like Tennyson, marsh sun on long wet sand
and I can't get out of my mind how from a habit of seeming concerned, though humble
he seemed safe enough to be queen's poet and voted her medal to Stevie Smith
as if any of the martyred Thomases might give a lunch to Simone Weil
how odd it was, being him, to publish poems less good than Eliot's and Auden's
knowing the quality wasn't quite there, and I like very much his wanting to be able
to write about anything, make putting a key in a door, buying a subway ticket romance
fit subject with a pretty adjective, as if fronting the ocean made one eventually a sea captain
and I can't but think, looking at people like him and thinking of the result
that it does, the big secret that the Bar can be crossed longitudinally.

My One Latin Poem

The need to be literate got me six lines of a nonextant poem by any of them,
mouthfilling like a Mexican cart, the wheels made of tree
or Barbara standing in the woods somewhere talking to badgers, fairies
visiting vertical words, holm oak and mushroom circlets as of rings
in streams, moist air on bluejeans or skirt a pledge that these are real.

It all drips, like some St. Trinian's child taking her hoop to the woods
the trees like dictionaries in rows (oh urbanity), even street lights in her verse
vegetable, vees of saltshakers in the sky, honking. You plump us like a Madras pillow
and bring us rhizomes under a cloth in your basket, smelling of bread.
It may be badgers believe in God but it was Stafford who wisely said
the insides of stones need our prayers, ending a stanza, and you belong
in that company of carter-poets, and those others la Woolf imagined, silent daughters
(Ms. Bronte mute, Dickinson illiterate) who'd think such things, looking at broom
and have the words, really have them, vanishing at one end still forming
at the other like dust on a doorframe or scones for tea privily in kitchen, so much
more to the point than cobbler for neighbors, with a note.

Word Fear

Enough of thinking, let us to the woods enow
like animals enjoy furry nakedness and eat chewy nuts
good alike for digestion and megrim. The language has
another, leering, over its shoulder like a standard character in Al
Ackerman's mail art, "hebephrenic," he says, speaking debased tongues
flawlessly, as if inside his system some born peasant almost himself pre-verbal
feels over *his* shoulder the speech of anyone. Squirrels and tree limbs
in wind chatter at him, the thongs with which he ties his pants too
much like writing, his bane, and the barn owls look wise, full of saws.
The point of the pastoral is imaginary shepherds' supreme verbality, wolves'
heads on forepaws listening, birds falling like pebbles from olive trees
and the purl of presumptive streams saying "a-rethoos, a-rethoos," even the
grating of tectonic plates on which your goaty islands white in glare shift
subtonically musical, wail of pan flute indeterminate.

Sex Fear

Torrentially, for instance, if one were to say torrentially rained on
the blandness of phrase would underlie (not overlay) some short clip, not still
of silver bluegray bashings up like curtain fringe of drops on asphalt, wet
bamboo. Just lately we saw the script for the silent film *Rain*
looking just as if it were all dialogue, blocked like any play, the rain
going on outside as it's read, or on tin roofs in jungles when it's shown
(the genius congratulatable who lashed Banana Republic iron, then played
Astaire through speakers like potted aspidistra), Ms. Sadie lurching out in satin
unaccountable in Malaysia the rough beast slouching toward clergymen
who blame it all on rain, for whom it *means* so much more, you see, irregular
liaisons, than it could to her—them—her, stand-in for everything, Gyges ring
conferring on its owner invisibility, through to graysuited ones in Indiana reading
Shandy in attics—I found in New York the last vivid audience for Anatole France,
not far from where Edward Dahlberg lived on eighty-oddth—treelined convention a rain
for them, alcoholic choirmasters in love with the more intelligible Browning, the gorilla
so coarsely shaggy its hair is a kind of green on the screen making off with blondes
Wray and Mae, Harlow dyeing her hair red for a particular part overlaying platinum

sighing for the later effect of Dietrich's curls appearing under the gorilla head lifted like a
tea cosy off hers, and you can imagine all through this the rain going on
all our roofs, sounding like the shutter's flutter you'd eventually wish away, even Lucas,
Spielberg, Allen, those in-love-with-love types tired of its predictable susurrus, word even
Pound's hard put to make love to, telling us that any outpost is lonely, the gin its
effect on film a light shines through, dulling to narrative, our collars, our satin dresses
a bravery made of self-pity, nostalgic for shops, and if I hand you a glass the gesture
registering as intended makes script a tawdry symbol of fate, our glory how the tawdriness
lived into, cloth creasing, soft pads of simian fingers on glass, then and only then
eyes meeting, bodies' felt length, nakedness a metaphor for getting free of cloth
too moist (metaphorically overfamiliar) without hope but all the top line script merely.

Image Fear

It's up to you to invent brocade, stiff cloth intruded on or crusted, metallic
thread's little dams to hold mirrors, these then made into puffy sleeves
or round fey caps. To wear them is like wearing a derby, a sign you
chose the stiffest convention, umbrella with ribs, thistletube hookah.
The country which permits this will undulate, or create in its
underground tramways the effect of undulation, land like the Downs traversed
by engine, underadored woman, unstiff, gold coins at the tummy ajingle, motile dowry
by meccano, the coin going back to its original state as jewelry, thing never
given away at all. Microprocessors in boxes are black marketware, like coffee
or greyhound pups for racing, poor man's afghans. We want it true that docks
now bombed revealed, opening in flame, splendid Fu Manchu apartments, perhaps
packed up, ghosts of splendor, here on the floor a bangle, marmoset dropping.
We reveal in these things a childish imagination, plotted by Stevenson, undone
desires, the kind boys like, and it took the author of *Swallows and Amazons* years
in Russia, experiencing Dnieper, to render children setting out in boats with fish paste
    sandwiches,
ginger beer (in "stone" bottles, wounding the mind with dreams of hollowing out) and that
    Sinister
Street character remembering chewing iron bedstead enamel mightn't have got far from
that initial state. It's now a custom to layer artfully broken thick glass with glue or bolts
the light can make the edges of green as you want, at the expense of its being sharp. Virginia
Woolf's father would write the history of each of those clergymen whose hobbies duplicate
these sermons in glass, unwished for shapes. Making anything is like having a vice,
leaving the door open deliberately in icy L——, knowing some connish traveler,
coming in, welcomed (comedy of denying the intent to burgle), waking from sleep under
    brocade,
feeling nearly one's way to the mirror, bigger than the wall needs, and in it
the room repeated, bed with chest at its foot, candle standard seven feet if it's an inch,
its smoky blue wick the common light, all, all mirrored except ourselves, the object of
the narrator's attention, anchor gone faceless, bodiless, sleeves of our shirt *there,*
smell of night and candle, taste of the odd wine proffered in a stone cup
by the host of antique lineage whose pleasure it was as announced to see to us, knew
our fictions, never announced passion for his daughter, longhaired, reminding us of she,
cousin, we played with diving into crystal waves, childhood an island of rugs on mottled
    green tile

we float on still, pull strength from as along pulled glass hairthin pipettes, to see by
    schoolroom geometry
the trick, the glass unsilvered, room in front of us not virtual but real, identically furnished
    in reverse.
A fish in round glass jar might similarly, tinted reddish orange, take over the idea of itself,
from moving round and round inside the painter's mind revolving oil, watercolor to a *series* of
atrocities which are the making conventional of live and prime uncarrotlike fish, inedibly
    untoward.

On His Fiftieth Birthday: Seven Poems

Superficial Gender

The early Anatolian figurine has breasts, discrete, conical
like an early teen, as if under a turtleneck, collar flared to a step
and perhaps an upper-face vizard (say leather) with eyes protruding
round, repeating the breasts but sideways to each other like a horse
(no other clothing indicated), penis like a stirrup pitcher handle, knees interrupting
pipestem legs (a few cracked places covered over, David says, with grit, the feet
turned in, gowky. Especially with Bettelheim's *Symbolic Wounds* on the table
at first it's a male pretending to be female with breastplate and birdlike goggles
then (looking at the knees, polished and blushing as a pre-teen's) a female pretending
to be male, that penis so last-minute attachable, assuming that's to say that gender
is an issue here at all in a figure perhaps seven inches long. We are seven. We're
in drag, we wear the requisite dildo. Who could care. No lust for origins need make us
fret like Frazer for sacrifices dimly imagined, something in Tennyson (our poets
of the subject seem only able to record the current fantasia, what's that
horned gent, so lithe on the Boston Museum cylinder seal doing, front hooves up)
and the problem is repeated in the wax they made to make him (her), as if all
sexual characteristics are secondary, early trepanning a trial run sex-changery.
(Who knows what will come out when humans try to make things literal?) Carrington letters
to Lytton or the boy-friends loathing menses could use this figure as paperweight,
willing to take on with shy intrepidity whatever the gender you want on it
accepting with its lyric knees and pigeon feet an almost reptilian disregard for iconography
of sex, testicles as epaulets, curving indentation in cool plum as much scrotum fissure as
bland hint that there are, in the least likely of surfaces, covert vaginas, as if bronze
in the casting would crystallize obediently into backup organs
(the point is) not even indicated on the surface figure, preserved for the time
parts and parcel, as in a Donatello Mercury one knows from any given lump the
woven muscle over rib, what it would feel like, to the sculptor's thumb.

Serial Monets

Ice floes at Bennecourt, the gray Rouen, odd mountain
(sky nearly bare), the Amherst Seine and Edinburgh's Grainstacks, the effect
like postage stamps on gray or green-blue walls, frames mostly staid, signature
Claude Monet most times the darkest use of paled down vermilion, orange, purple, bluish
    green

sometimes disguised as grass, rock, or writing floated on a painting, morningglory morning
   suns
like navels in Rouen. One paints, and in that way "gets to be" a painter.
These pictures are of not very movable places, the bend of a river, a cathedral
and you are there more than once, striking a note or not (often, in winter, blandest
vermilion dissolved in white right at the foreground) these really not very pretty fetal
   headlands
made, in one instance, unfortunately in a private collection in Switzerland, exquisite—
   gather of
birds left, brush-flicks, the same right in umber paint for what, also in air, the same birds
in a different light? I hoped so. Light doesn't really dissolve or render things transparent
though on water it can shine through a battleship, reduce the bobbing float to wave-flick
and as we know from British ads the Ripper walks in mist cut with glycerine.
It's treating air by water as a sister element that gets him half of these, coastal Vétheuils
with hollyhocks. There are dark darks under far thickets you can indicate with a line or two
that would be middle values in somebody else's painting. The nicest river-island trees
is a gray one from Philadelphia with the icy shoreline more indicated than usual, partly in
the raw blue Picasso used to suggest feet on his Demoiselles. Outside a lovely Chase
"Gray Day" in a Venetian bay, impossibly liquid paint being sky, packetboats, a dome.
Our Monet when he isn't making a thick pile like a motel rug to thickenize Rouen
will make large swipes on foregrounds, remembering himself as he retreats (so unlike
   Whistler's
technique, say, in "Last of Old Westminster," factory chimneys orangely bright, exactly
   right)
and we are in this heaven of inexact exactitude, not at all Gauguin but rain and steam
visibilized by equally chancy means, the up-color Japanese Bridge in Houston
(not in this exhibit) in which reds and purples, infinitely expensive reddish browns,
all right from the tube or just the right touch of pastel drag over each other like
tortellini reheated badly to make this singing jewel-like casket with in it somewhere
a bridge our quondam friend told us (he's been to Giverny) is really small
hence even here the viewer so ready to give in, accept as leaves these lines
or pale blue dot low down "sky" or "lily," looking to him like it looked
like something you can be sure looked to him like something like that looked to him
this viewer, looking at this thing, perhaps getting the scale wrong (isn't the scale
of anything in a rectangle always correct?) might mistake some of these blobs
for Chase's bleeding harbor ships but doesn't. We are told in Turner to look
for the hare in flight before the train and see it, little browny smear, obediently as Turner's
   hare.
A few of the duller headlands are signed the way you know he'd sign a bank check,
something for the syndics, those wanting a genuine enough Monet, but a never to be
   mentioned
consequence of returning *over* and over to a motif's the relief of painting badly
now and again, this cliff like a red cabbage with AIDS, ghastly taxgatherer's hut
and this is part of what you do if paint flows by you, canvas spates, this stratagem
whereby a placecard in Tennyson's hand ends up on Geoffrey Hill's wall, arrested script.

The Perfect Rock

The rocks you see in crocks holding up azaleas, at the borders of rose and iris beds
may be doubly found, tumbled by glaciers to globes, tomahawkshaped flat wedges
you know some neolith spent years looking for, kept in a woven grass or leather bag
at belt, not edged but heavy enough for odd whacking, already pre-formed,
the work done for you, just the right shape, so you carry it around, minor swellings
become familiar, incorporated into one's feeling of "perfect," the weight better and better,
felt as counterpoint to bag against the thigh, guarantee, and it is *your* stone,
your finding it a part of its prefabrication. And as you pass further gravel heaps,
points of ground with rocks in, you keep looking while this does not at all put in question
your having found the perfect rock. I could have two tools, you think, or imagine the
three-stone Y you throw to trap a thing with genteel legs—months of plaiting, then
practice—but ultimately prefer your rock, warm from the hand or sitting (daringly
unleashed, mistakable on the ground for a free rock, any old thing, rubble) so when
after years of hitting things successfully you move away, find a better rock or die
it's played with a bit or chucked, given the children as important, buried with you
and in the evolution of ages surfaces again it's here, the same rock, only apparently
     historyless
but weight and curves containing the old appeal for hands of a size, not underspecialized
for propping, tapping, whacking husks off, putting in a straightsided fluted soufflé dish
to hold long stems of yellow flowers, two or three to a cluster, that rock, the one near me
like the one I saw in the garden, more a hatchet maybe, greener, but the same appeal not to
the hand but to the eye, not felt adequation but a message promising it, a hope of it.

Another Pebble

fractures sick in the center like the heavy round
ones we saw like crystallized gunpowder in the
New Age shop that're supposed to go to nothing,
discreate, if struck wrong or something, the
median line around strong, as on the quite large
hailstones that falling once at SMU, catchable out
Dallas Hall's georgian windows this sometimes wavy
seam (like a sea-cucumber's side stripe) had me
thinking about faults, the Fall, Lucretius, just
from holding this translucent chunk that if candy'd
taste of wintergreen, well Michael these rocks of
yours in garden beds are that for me, incipiently
split. Ponge's *Pebble* comes from cliff face, more of
these in MacDiarmid's *Stony Limits,* as if anything not
Da Rock itself has in it shear, acknowledgment of
parametric frangibility, as Tim Coursey used to grieve
at the Army .45, almost a definition of the window in
which, unmelted, uncrystalline, saturated with partisan
relief it might be said to function, otherwise machine
oil turned to jelly, brass and copper expanding at different
rates till like a toy tin pistol run over in the streets
it's futile wafer, Jekyll without principle, Hyde without lust,
its holster a business envelope. My own variant, probably

still in Somerville asphalt, on the Figure of Outward's a
soda can near the bus depot so much a monstrance for all
happened-on virtue even its photo . . . And you, knowing
the tone, will believe without proof, the grumble of gravel
if not in any bag you carry then all over your private desk
and alcove surfaces, found stones obscuring white paint, mahogany,
habit like a child's of bringing outdoor things inside, that
maybe moves us to pick up washers or slugs, bolts in U shapes,
hollow metal half-balls recessed in squares, run-over necklace
chains and hook earrings, square nails, used car fuses so like
phials, the perfect moulded taillight ruby plastic shells, too
common silver paperclips, often large, wires with flat connectors,
coins (never foreign, though I did once find a Dallas Transit
Token under matting), these flakings off, as if of incandescent
metal from giant steel rhombi, or Brunetto's skin in Dante, off
monolith company factories on their sides huddling crystalline
out of the ground, not unwanted, not tristely discarded like an
infant or cast-iron inkstand for which you've now something
Napoleonic, and not like less-needed words, *buhl, marchpane,*
not even like (say) rhetoric imagined as the giant calipers and
magnetic cranes to push around scrap steel, cubed cars, otherwise
valuable—no, not these, even, not anything hidden in the
assumption *struktur,* but more like Aristotle's wise remark that
anything which can fall apart will, that *if* the substance you're
fond of has in it anything, not necessarily "fracture," it will
fracture, the shear plane no matter how surprising already
indicated (as, say, snake's poison) by a kind of belt or maybe
just orientation suggesting middle, something for grasping hands,
avoiding, to posit as where it will open or unscrew, some urban
notion that not everything needs bashing. Those Japanese boxes
may likewise be in essence no more than that twist with which
strong hands might break an apple, cleanly, seeds laid bare
but pebbles aren't genes. Carolee Schneemann's live-in lizard
is "green" by total bodily guilt but made of pinkish mauves,
grays, anything lizard that, as if enlarged, makes green, the
eye, blacker than any seed, sloe, aged date, contemporary in
elbowed body under fluorescents yet, in outline, Jurassic chunk.
I suspect your generic abstracts, I-any-I looked OUT (any) window
as ahh wahlked ahht, with morning like a flatiron in tailor window
so like a relic of tailoring, I, looking out the way my ancestors
have done, looked out, I S A W a pebble hacked from the larger
cliff of things described as having been seen, as if medievals
catching themselves up might write A VISION OF VISION to be
maybe what the tailor also needs, a brick through the window,
flash-gilt iron snatched (as if one might run away with the giant
kettle downtown sign that really steams), which is to say one
non-electric (nowadays unusable) flatiron exchanged for one brick,
the modern critic right if he proposes you keep roles (the tailor
is the audience) but next time the poet heave the iron through
the window, steal the brick. Prometheus mocks any sort of notion
that poetry's a mountain, preexistent, out of which you chisel bits
or "flame" if that for you is element, Bachelardian fire—red
from strontium nitrate—your arbolast throws in their rigging,

all these still coming down to this wee souvenir rock, presumably
rounded, not the ones with sharp-sharp edges like fine foam rubber
snipped into cubes, I mean the suckable lollipop stones one thinks
of, saying "pebble," no reason not for them to be cast bronze or
dried chestnuts except a residual sense of probity Samuel Johnson
may have tried (knowing he'd fail) to bully *out* of one, plain as
a rock, plain as that. I like it that they take on stains, alter
by porosity, in that sense open, before some tendril chisels in,
and that a handful click and rattle like my lithomantic eight, now
nine, from my inclusion of a black one found in the Santa Fe street
where all the galleries meet, painters and sculptors having asked
us there, not writers, and there I was, thinking what was cast up
at my foot might not, after all, mean my death, in any case fit
for the event. So far, if you're interested, I've cast it once.

The Romance of Print

Take, you always want to be saying, and perhaps it's a signature, the person hands full of
    jewels saying here
donations even of Constantine, untoward nature saying no, not everything's on display but
    you can
have, experience this, a starfish on the beach, its foam, prickly slowness, everything in the
    world
a whatnot, left in place there not necessarily *for* us, but we collaborate in finding it, the sand
around moist, compacted, and I hate all this hurruff, poling my skiff under the Opera, their
    bass
my baritone, no question but living with papier-mache mock people, Daleks, swans with
    gold wings
—my andirons Egyptian tomb dogs, even a perfectly made sphere tending to look period.
Tell these stories in smudged print because once kings liked to hear them sung, my
Papillon shaking her head as my pen writes. I knew clowns who'd love finding giant
    ballpoint pens
because so much the thing for giving autographs to children, and think of him passing
window-length pencils in Bob Slate's (how ya doing, Hi Fi), putting my cup
with catspaw fleurs-de-lys on Mackey's *Bedouin Hornbook,* the *Phantom* over
on Michael Franco's telly. It takes him a long time to read things so it doesn't do
to write *for* him, like cooking for a very fat person. One afternoon spent
printing ads for Robert Kelly's reading will be enough: Michael, having cut the linoleum
    block
and spread paste ink in stripes on a glass plate, a dark inky blue, bright red and viridianish
    green
rolls these flatter with a huge aluminumhandled brayer, giant platen
which then he runs *diagonally* to ink the plate
so the stripes aren't vertical. A bit of paper on, just touched to till it catches ink,
stack of thick oil-paper buffer sheets then rolled under the heavy press, cast-iron
or something honeycombed, he starts or else I pull the long handle till pressure
catches it, then through to the end, six-second pause (unspoken prayer for ink to penetrate)
back with the arm, watching it doesn't snap the last small way, told
the separator left off deliberately lets the whole heavy power-communicating mechanism
fall right out, shop steward yelling you've ruined the press, big joke

but we've another, yet another Kelly flyer with bold leaves in blue or green
like a Mexican skirt, tail end of Carmen Miranda's design sense, drying on one another
toward an event half a month off. I was fifty in this house (I think that day)
good enough use to make of it, the rollers, brayers, lino block wiped with kerosene, white gas
in rags now plum-black that go in a nickeled waste can, posters for to be
put up when I am gone. In Santa Fe I saw for the first time how to make the printer's cap
from text you've worked on, the flyer for a poetry reading too small even for a clown's.

Medieval Assumptions

These languages are free from reference, hence pure, disjunct additions to the "world"
of print, like a collage made of magazines printed in a magazine, something new everyone's
seen before,
the demonic element to this, thing shouldering up from Themis cave, the mica flakes and
sulfur smell
guarantee authenticity, "tell" us everything, as a mask's cone mouth is always speaking,
some
hiss off the cylinder, between us a motive for language still in air, like the possibility of
compassion at the scene of an accident, strobe flashes on policecar tops less personal, less
revolved.
So gimmicks abound, you think of some slum kewpie with windup mechanism in its tummy
and there again
the double-A battery subverts your image, writing instrument a laptop as the basketball or
something player (between
autographs) pulled up the memo function in his briefcase on the plane, flat screen propped
up on his large knees
our urge here's to live an old life lapped in the new, watch on the wrist more complex than
time itself
and you fly into it in the fantasy film and it's gears, escapement (that medieval triumph) so
when it
bongs it's release, no teeny quartz vibrating given juice, thing for Marianne Moore to think
of as cubes
like maybe what the tongs release to tea, or nail scissors curving accurately around the
glacier's perimeter
for the collage with tiger, some dark melanchthal elephant and pangolin, flitterbat
cut through by steeple, another "world" the critics say, thing with demonstrable foyer, our
church in Brooklyn with its pastor coming through the pointed door like Death in Holbein,
Laughton
plump as a gremlin forcing open copper gargoyle jaws, ecclesiastic impedimenta as proper
toy, my
crow, Pluto, the brutally asserted familiarity with nonintensive recognizable we're to find
ordinary
swimming like Swinburne in maternal surf of bald assertion, this building if you call it edifice
rhymes with this. Meanwhile (Franco knew a poet whose "but" meant, every time, what I
just said was garbage)
the limit here is not patience with the poet but with the world. Still, political commitment
is contained
inside language's, as fair's included as a special (aberrant) instance in justice, the judge's
horsehair wig

her living in (as if a diving helmet, or choosing to be a stable for) truth, the ornament that
   works, Gargantua's
churchbells filched to make a horse's bridle ding.

In Codrescu's Corpse

Matthew Wills is wonderful on *2000 Maniacs* as what the south was thought to be
when it was still capitalized (as it is here by copy editor David Racine), dwelling so
gratefully on lost detail like fingering the Buick portholes while deliberately *not* feeling
   nostalgic I'm
suspicious of the whole joyous greeting of the crude. Just today I saw, driving around lost
   in San
Antonio a star, sort of tin-colored or maybe oil shale but a star, smaller than a pieplate by a
dull-colored house front door, thrust out from it an angled pole, on it the Lone Star flag, no
particular day just general patriotism. My heart lep up. Less than a month back I took my
canvas bag of paint to the Austin capitol, a building taller than imaginable if you're used to
   Washington,
and found I'd no drier, no medium at all, just raw paint in tubes. I poked a stick into the ground
and tied one easel leg to it, another to my jackhandle (it was windy) and started a
   near-white grayish sky
laid on in flat smears. Trouble with oil right out of the tube is it's stiff, and stays wet forever so
new paint on top of old just slides (or mixes), everything wanting to be everything else,
   went on
with lots of white because the day was overcast, and finished the damned thing with just a few
outliney touches for the statue to the left, and cannons, pillars on the dome, some of the
   lovely
windows half shut with what looked like pull shades. People'd come by to look at the
   monument
I had my back to, say how nice my painting was, go away. No one stayed to see it through
but me; painting's not really a performing art except for a video of Helen Frankenthaler
   at the
Fort Worth show, laying it on the raw canvas with longhandled sponge mops as if to *2001*
   docking music
and a lovely show that was too. I'm willing to allow the violence, fear of the south in its
   capital, and remember
for instance a black neighbor James Hillman had over to some backyard event in Dallas
   who,
questioned urbanely and certainly politely about how Texas was got downright nasty, from
   drink or vividness of recollection
of being pushed off the sidewalk and so on by any white fart, somehow more impressive in
   this setting
of low voices, educated Texans among whom this man was certainly a welcome temporary
   presence. Carolee Schneemann
remembers (checking barrels for wine) coming on radio parts cached toward the
   *bund*rising, ja, and you
may recall in Griffith the finding of the KKK robe like George Washington holographing
   into Hitler
and I agree with Mr. Wills that violence is there, sexually awake, in what Presley did with
   black

material, his blueness suede (you wait for him to conk someone, reveal his trooper nature)
   oh acrylic
clocks shaped like guitars in restaurants, the cat-eating idiot next door raising his voice in
   what he
thinks is song (that he'd not do if it weren't for, a long way back, such models), that it's here
in any flag, sectional or not if Jim Crow no longer jumps in secondary schools, but the south
is no more black and white than Jekyll and Hyde is or are, united by the y hidden in the
   name
like some dinner they serve the whites in Monticello (the cellar or garden-flat cells under
   tink
of chain and banjo) and we cull herbs, hide deep the sharpened spoon, Virginia's latifundia
a prison like a ship, powered by horses hauling things up its giant hill, imagined like the
   clock weights going
down through the floor not *up* to the (vacant, unused) dome. The aristocratic south is its
   cellarage,
some of Poe here, but riding too and shooting birds so accurately you try, finally, to remove
just the top of the brain-pan. Mike and Missy Clark's lions thirty miles north of Dallas, now
on tour in Texas, that he'll beg with a Regency bow to come off their perches and Carolee
   just called to say
she's photographed the iguana and its image in the mirror, the tongues in a way kissing.
The south is not like palm trees in the west of Ireland, gulf stream epiphenomenon, but as
   David Searcy says
the dogwoods, out in April, are in wooded areas like clouds of insects seen through trees,
   history scuffed
like a one-volume Portable Gibbon, this urge to tell everyone what history *is* ultimately not
   southern, telling
a story even on one's own grandfather, what seems an obsession with history here really
   often
an obsession with family. Myth in the south is always a myth about relation.
There is no myth of the south.

Another Rose Poem

Roses, the best roses. Carolee was choosing a characteristic postcard for Fredericksburg,
picturesque farm building, perfectly authentic with in the front not roses but big red flowers.
A magnifying glass in the Birdhaus section (with curved porcelain handle with birds on)
   showed
in wavery expansion the foreground bed pure Hollywood, definitely munchkin,
in my mind Plath's red poppies in the hospital room, stealing her breath,
Searcy's "Metaphor" dead on the beach, throat choked *full* of old roses
and we are again in Metaphorland, where any dandelion's a rose, and roars
like MGM. Back from the copy shop a nice dwelling with white iron trellises
framing entryway, woman placing begonias or something, reddish-rose sticking out
from fleshy leaves sticking out, one at each side, so beautiful I said so.
I don't choose to write a poem about roses. Our dog walked in the botanical garden
showed the ivory ones there ate them, embarrassing as if a child did something out of place
yet confirming edibility of petal, evolved endive. We just retrieved
from my parents' house a painting of roses in a wire-locking jar, peach and rosecolored
   ones, bouquet
done too quickly waiting for Harlen Welsh to come help with the computer,

rendering harmonic dissonance of fleshcolored buds and rose, that the flower is a color
a pleasure and a puzzle. Green roses would be interesting; Goethe'd approve.
That any flower is in fact a rose is proved by the old mindreader's trick, name
a color (red), a flower (rose) so often, as if any animal's a dog. This season
everywhere, on the highway, in overgrown yards, bluebonnets, seeping by way of
Germanic turn of the century nature painters onto plates, postcards, beady earrings
and these too are roses, the Texas Yellow Rose is blue.

The Late Pest

It's always there, that lump Levertov said like dough on baking-day oppresses
the reader's stomach, AIDS as much as the war presenting itself to those who haven't it
as if too old for the draft, too sexually inactive, not nicked in surgery as a
problem in how to hold yourself toward. Pepys or Defoe'd describe whole cities vacated,
people throwing naked teens out of attic windows (the lower ones boarded), that huge
X in paint, do not bring in like a Welcome Wagon casserole some evidence that
Saint Joan, offered file pie, refused. In any case it's from the judges' view, as Poe's
"Pit and the Pendulum" is oddly the torturer's, settled somehow on the victim like a net of
    gnats, thing
too confusing to shake off, that disorientation that comes from thinking of villagers as less
    than enemies
but rats, for all their majesty of form, as carriers, so in "King Pest" it's rats as much
as bellied flagons (like some Fritz Kredel-illustrated Rabelais) that tears us up by showing us
the frank glance is false, achievable by the genuine ingenuousness of love or schizophrenia
and sympathy playing cards in the hellcat's mouth vulgar as a Fun House. Enter it.
This mirror makes your buckle, sixties ban-the-bomb rocketly thirded, aging angel
    beerbrand or Remington
as handkerchiefs tucked out, keys at the belt, pentagram in silver ring propose meaning,
we find down steps the forgotten city, as in the television series vampires under San Francisco
remember Prague, and Eva Hoffman's usably imagined memoirs of being lost in language,
    between languages
—move—us tied so elastically to ours, oval though the circles we describe may be.
It's description that's at risk, not just our bodies too, the blood in that beautifully
lit lab equipment ours, not ours, peeling posters advertising the passé, the problem that
a different time is felt to be imposed, as Sontag in the Boston library, New York in boots
read that thing about how one might come to be something or other, dyed in a
problem rather than concerned and it doesn't matter, that too fine as driving the heaped
carts is fine or sharpening stakes, or getting wine on the cards already, you see,
tainted with bacilli, what fun he'd have had with a microscope, the germ a gene.
Some plexes do radiate, others brighten a haze never really defined, as one wants
to concentrate a crayfish, ghost, Klein bottle on black velvet by means of an opaque
projector onto dense fog but wonders how and in what aspect it holds up, this image
of image as involved in a physicality of doubt why we've trouble with what strikes down
celebrities. No wonder the Death figure rising out of the ground, this bone buffoon
is how the peasants thought of it, or were taught by Epinal woodcuts to think they thought,
indulge the free reckoning like carousers in the rifled cellar, rats in the vat
swimming or drowning, our concern so far in a way from our concern, the gap-toothed
being with the rent tummy pops another cork, losing another tooth so doing, Warhol's
    lovely transvestite

losing one in an apple a sign, that pensive look despair polished, and we put
on a blue velvet cloth what we've collected, nail, button, nickel under puddle water, for
    luck.

Protecting the Face

The which is nature's iamb and doth grow in Spenser lanes all innocent
as fits a vegetable of no earthly use to man; we have our "you" sealed up
in Robert Peters's criticism like a cigarette in a glass vial for abstainers,
emergency pronoun, shapes agreed on as permissible in schools that teach you verse
as if there were a patent hamburger flavored with vanilla eaten only by people who do
you teens so glib on ordering one's funeral, whose flowers are from a florist
the duck mask I found in the street today, glaring eyes and blue puff cap, impossibly complex
beak with tiny printed instructions: 1. Fold bill up to face. 2. Hold bottom and
fold bill down to form visor. 3. Adjust to size using tab. has its tongue out, lacks
side pieces that would make it some horrible crown but these, along its ripped edges, you
    supply
along with what in grade school we were taught "is there" in sentences like these numbered
    ones,
the jussive "you," pronoun invisible, Sir Thou who beareth shield painted on the inside
so only he (or she, some with masses of hair inside the helmet, which tumble down to effect)
can see, the modesty underlying armor, amour, the which one may not put aside having had
    one's vigil
like Quixote in Doré, sitting up in the undershirt *by* one's armor in moonlight, horsetrough's
    hairthin worms
invisible, too fine for burin line but not necessarily inappropriate to the final hexameter
as Mutabilitie, a Titan, orders Cynthia (the moon) to abdicate, as if to say all change
would now be for the worse unlike (say) Jonson's Euphantaste whose crescent on a
    mercurial basin hat
means increase, Fowler's Lewis says in lecture notes on Spenser in which you find Venus's
    double nature
unveil'd, not so far after all from a child leaving the fast-food place or a party
wearing a duck, the visor folded by a parent in arcane ways, walking about like some
apotropaic boat, Minoan jar with octopi whose nouveau suckers are also eyes.

The Pebble in the Bell

Machado says the little doll with jingly thing in the belly is a toy, like planned obscurity
in a poem and in Gibbons's translation from his Spanish (the s's are different, all consonants)
I see, punch through to hand-moulded poppets the size of Russian mother-dolls with others
    inside
but made of dough or that substance they use for souvenir boots, strawberry clusters, cacti,
    anything recognizable
made into earrings, painted in colors bright to muddy, that clack a bit as you piece through
    them on the rack,
anyway this notion of breakable paste dolls with tummies that jingle as beneath the attention
    of the serious Spanish mind,

thing not (like obscurity) to put in poems, like a thimble in a cake, watch where you bite!
Maria having this V-shaped gap

in a front tooth from having found the ring, and she unmarried, Machado, your name begs
direct address

is there in your village nothing manmade on the ground for days too worthless to pick up?
dogs and

children have this knack for finding the perfect stick (like an old twelvepenny nail, square,
one end knobbed)

and I have seen old beer tabs fashioned into endless chains, yet I do not wish this poem to be

about garbage, the "patently useless discard" an old poem of mine says, writing from this
citadel of waste,

but rather simply the attitude of mind, proud of its cufflinks and white cuffs, addressing the
typewriter in a

port city, glass to hand with something citrine, while as you say *what makes* what you
write about

more valuable than the loaflike squares of imitation ivory (probably Dutch) your fingers
press—in

Spanish would it be "stamp"? to make this poem or letter on a pastel aerogram, space left
at left by

experience for the gummed tab that, coming below the fold extends, when you get to it,
the margin there, the

satisfaction of knowing all that, how to move among, what I mean as Stein used to wonder
that young men

dropped into offices swim about at once, carry paper, as if a gene for officiousness's innate.
Is it

with you, surrounded with Indio quaintness, protection against bready moulded kitsch or
is there on your chest

a ghost medal, smaller than a dime, a Christopher or Virgin in its ghost of gold, above the
sternum just below the breasts,

keeping you impatient with little mysteries left rattling in poems so you distinguish
Mallarmé's effects

from those things Mallarmé's effects evoke, the space between the neck and body magical
on the prisoner puppet,

separated by the soldier-puppet's sword, these gifts of assent to strings, to wooden sword,
the dummy's painted gaze and

trappy mouth not all our gift, Coleridge incorrect when he said we take but what we give,
his applegreen

sunset so much more gaudy in your country's gold trim, salmon accents aggressive as your
birds led the

conquistadored to leave niches in walls near the ball courts and pyramids for monkeys and
macaws when there were festivals,

as Crowley's when I was a child in downtown Detroit made displays at Christmas, soldiers,
bears, trains animate,

assembly lines like River Rouge and pointless activity, ballooning, perhaps bears writing
poems, such

pots of paint, the brushes moving up and down, skaters, whatever repetitive motion imitable
by cam, the jingle

in the belly of the doll at least this. Last month I drove past those windows (shuttered in
blackened greenish-brown)

and am pleased to report they were still doing that, persistent in the motion of their doing that.

Documentary Infusion

A floor covered with flimsies, pink, green, gray, arranged by color, the
year's finances, like some aerial county view Maxine Kumin could
write something homey about, not forgetting the horse's bones from an ampler farm,
reminded of miniaturizing bucolica less by my full-height view of it than stepping
Gulliverly over, between it all toward tea in the kitchen (roach bones under
the mat), the allocation of one's living to areas, feeling like
the Church of Ireland suddenly having to justify itself, government expense
for a filmy class's Sunday edification, black spike of St. Patrick's
imitating iron fences around holdings. At TCD I went through hundreds of
disestablishment pamphlets, pro and con, quickly produced on
paper you'd now use for wedding invitations, the paradox of cheap rag
taken up with tables (descriptions of the best pamphlets always involve tables)
and if you look closely at the journeyman type embodying ranked facts it
sticks up at you spikily like the name Malthus in caps and little caps
floating on the page like a Moon, midhigh, on this pure white rag
not at all foxed from residual acid as near-contemporary books were
and you think those rusty chaplains went on instinct to the more conservative
printers with stacks of this paper to throw in on either side
of a quarrel, thing balled up, chucked over the area railing,
slid into the *Times* on the front mat, Shelley's *Defence of Atheism* so conveyed
for the joy of their taking it in with the kippers or curried peas,
Newman wishing the bishops be granted holy martyrdom, so lovingly
in its thinness, thin as starched bands, or Pusey on Baptism,
the *damage* these things used to do. Where are (now) the dark
brown leatherette *Ego and His Own*s the Modern Library issued on
dusty gray paper back when Liveright owned it, or that earlier chunky printing
by (what was it) Freedom Press backed by that philanthropist,
this rudge of pamphlets since the *Acta Studiorum,* news of discoveries
which were, if anything, how they were taken up by readers
in whose minds these tables assume hymnal status by unbaptized infant tongues rehears'd
leading to action, press of numbers like the folios in Napier's *Letters*
on my mother's shelf, next to Sayers, Allingham, Deighton, Bailey, the
investigative Austin Freemans, *Red Thumb Mark,* depending on calibration
now with us, the gradual twisting of a loose heel rigid in caoutchouc.

Rosa Monstrosa

a meaning borne in her lecture's not *essentialismo*
has a thirty-foot painting of rocks, loveliest ochers with red around
in the middle, the blue around to the right, for with
a floor of rocks, another painting painting it self on the monitors
another one. Isolate as War Mop (mounted in clear acrylic kidneys,
whacking a telly's prettied atrocity, bombardment we funded. The green
rose, David says, *Rosa monstrosa,* frilly petals like carnations, is green,
brown in autumn. In a vase, a mouthful of alum. Women in the
audience (one redhaired one who, still in black, served me Guinness in the college pub)
assume the shapes. Of clear acrylic, curved tape pulled off canvas and
Monet-basement Orangerie thirty-foot rocks you'd want to walk

on if. Heavy earring's red-yellow-red stones on silver, trafficlight
's question, male vs. female batting averages on blackboards in polaroid
and Canright's largest pulled-away tape paintings gallery-free
(people'd "pull away") the fiddle shapes beautiful against les choses
projected on, this notion anyway of layering, pulling away or Liberty sheer,
how easily your substances accept themselves as like the hand, body,
Etruscan wedgy mirror people abraded there, "polish" a finer form.
Jan 1990 *Art in America* on O'Keeffe, Canright says, champagne over.
Kant figures make the plan a point of awe, win that way
space for the silver figurine on the board's maroon and drab off squares, under
it a slip of paper on which (a message) history is this, shadowed f-
holes on alabaster celli that. You take the historied
piece, with a history (ultimately always the zippered face) what was done
a cosmetic overlay, sign that it was. The bull fiddle head
in the Cafe Concert, hairs on that wrist, stay with us like a photograph
of a dog you forgot you had. Ruskin's condemned for writing of Venice
ignoring Oxford. Alleys take light imperfectly semiotically.
The choice of work, what to do, redefines
ultimately the "what," its part of speech, that an action
isn't one until a wisp of word, the sprite a fact
heads off theory, the thick goat hide a thick goat.

II

Hemiptera likewise emerald's dream of jade, build in their tent,
whole body a flanged pebble tool, fat pod for one long pea
and the flea, mad thing, is likewise vertical
so you can go through life, live frontally, towering
over all with a hump that in larvae cuts
open the egg like a gelatin capsule, is not
trapped inside.
The shadow you cast is larger side-lit. The dollar
coin insufficient gnomon, one's back a cello.
Crouch, leap, the goat you are always a tendency
to pull in like a shrimp toward a center,
complete something that if it were would be
of no account. It's like being responsible
for the wordless text of your performance piece,
potted thing sickening on mulch or burned
by raw manure a lesson to the amateur, orrible
example. In rectories in quite unpleasant places
they wrote verse on Timbuctoo, made tiny booklets on
imaginary places, grew to be Charlotte, Emily, write
their novels, the unwritten one *The Female Laureate*.
Sneered at by Larkin, pitied by Woolf, there's as you
say a time that doesn't matter, even in the pupa
stage of having-made. It comes, Pirandello says,
to eyeglasses, folding lorgnettes you evolve, have
chosen for their ornament as what symposiasts wear
as carapace is ours to act on. Imagine Emerson saying
inside the grandest preacher's this *Poltergeist III*
roundheaded grub (a critic) you can, by feeding it
royal jelly, turn into a poetess. Who hangs the curtains

in Poe Cottage might take his "Philosophy of Furniture"
to heart though sure to bury a trick one (inflating like
a jokeshop Plate Lifter or vegetable lung sacs in *The Thing*)
under the puncheon flooring, nostalgic as hair in a locket.

The Dixie Salon

amuses with accounts of males calling with deals, insisting on speaking to the husband
ten years deceased (one said, "I spoke to him in January," told the truth, "Well, I might
have been mistaken, *click*") anecdote sliding in the mind like dominos just out of
the box nostalgic for mah jong, the point being a cool drink booted with mint grown
eighty feet away like a largish rose leaf of the sort my quondam jewelry firm
would vend, gilt for wearing on a thin chain, say something eighteen-inch I see
still on people in offices, public transport, thinking it less a wanting to wear jewels
than the acknowledgment the shrub's a thing to wear, the garden on the body. Our
generosity, no matter a bitterness of underflavor, takes on the form of anecdote like leaves or
Simon David bagboys in green ties and aprons, grandeur genuinely genuine, pace the
      vegetables
swept up in the back halfway to mulch. We recognize as a virtue that the face is a facade, gift
like the Chicago building Clio was reading about, walls pierced metal, marble and ship
      lanterns, church
for commerce, even the slabs of brown-gray marble in Harvard upper-house shower stalls
I'd spray with disinfectant and wash down the memory that there was Caracalla,
corroded flanges realest brass underneath nickel. I suppress, here, the sinks of South
      Americans.
Comus walks her dog (disguised) past our porch. A cat with three legs nobbles on. Squirrels
in the gutter attest to gravity. It's not at all that the ordinary here is mythic (an Agatha
Christie, classic shape, lent this morning) but that storiness itself is more acceptable, legend
corroding to show beneath the pits solidarity of honest brass, Birminghamese transmuting
      it, by use, to gold.

Pungencies of April

It's not not-horse, sitting here smelling a slight odor of dung
not from old jeans, old shoes that walk the dog in grass, nor any
disobedience on polished flooring. It is more (Stevens) a memory this moist day
of circuses in Butte, Boise, Kalispell, the time it rained in North Platte, the
organist employing clothespins on her music; granular feel of half-froze
horsemeat for the beasts (so much preferred to frozen chicken—remember always
the hunger of animals caged for shipping and exhibition, elephants and llamas
in this respect no different from the dog act (now dispersed), Miss Liberty
or something tutued, blare of trumpet at fiestaware, the chimps rewarded with
hot chocolate, vegetables in supermarket discard via Vespa, all these produce the
prairie smell of pachyderm, felidae high-protein's nitrogenous waste (sometimes a
black ichor like tar, hard to wash off), Hi-Fi's rooster all red and green no doubt
producing something, travel reducing in a way to this municipal concern with
propagation of dung, as Poor-Law Commissioners agents rooting about in ghettos found a

kind of paralytic dazed inability to shift the mounds of human excrement obscuring cobbles
and crossing-sweepers to keep long trousers and skirts from fouling established fords
of more or less navigable paving, and necessary-men like camels with their shapeless sacks
    of straw
left, probably, trails like those to Djibba, and sinkers of cores in ash-pits begin to find
styrofoam and plastic dissolved but paper, ah, remains, partly from layeredness, the constant
discovery in Egypt of yet more Menander dull but all Aristotle buried in a cellar,
Sappho disjunct like amulets tucked here and there on mummies, among them the
sexton beetle, scarab, resurrection-bug, shown in *Scientific American* to move carpets of
    ordure
from elephant encampments overnight. So we're reminded that our waste, imperfectly
processed garbage (sound now of alley truck collecting ours) appeals to us as faces imagined
    as familiar,
Lamb's dream-children, that which was not also, in our wing chair, what was's inhalation
the touch of perfume in a string-drawer bland yet challenging evidence of life mislaid.
Seed corn I saved from feeding deer and, rather than throw out, planted by the garbage cans
comes up in shadow, furled spears living off dog pee and limestone soil.

Ancient Mysteries Unraveled

Azoth then, or something like it, crude white lead from zinc vanes buried in dung, anything
    sticky
ambient medium for the poor sad platinum wire, which even when Eliot wrote his absurd
    comparison
was known to be, chemically, very active, providing a skim of electrons as the plunger in a
    metal
kid's toy rotates the wheel, eroding flint. The great Canadian plate, like a bald
spot, something not to be got to belches, peers past us to spot the drinks, the scene
again of one so sunk in rote creation it's too late to offer gifts, new chalk.
We beg their attention, give Chaplin his Oscar, Oona full of narrative about her father.
Beerbohm photographed as Whistler's Carlyle keeps one hand idly on the absurd peaked hat
memory by Le Gallienne gone sideways, bowl of milk with a raisin or two from bran
too long in the icebox also self-portrait. (Danson prints one, young, looking like Alec
    Guinness
with a boutonniere of sealing wax, very proper invasion of cardboard by wit,
reams of anecdote unneeded to enforce a standing.) I've drawn a heavy
jeaned young man, bearded, opening a fortune cookie like a hunter watch, fringed subeditor
peering in the Chinese restaurant sack, on the wall a calendar, a Wyoming stamp
overprinted by the government with PROPORTIONS and, half-legible against ink peaks,
    STAMPS!
and something like the root of a buffalo horn stuck in a cabbage, called The Editors of
    Exquisite Corpse
Apologize, on the desk top a few papers held down by a skull. The best descriptions
of paintings, in Allingham's *Death of a Ghost* and H. C. Bailey's gallery story (the face in
    glory, and diabolical addition)
please as the mysteries about actors must please actors. The Camera Club Murders. The
imagined corpse ages for the first few chapters, pending discovery. It's then photographed
from all angles, solved by a print. Some few postwar had sketches the detectives drew.
One could look long at the iris in the Dell paperback keyhole logo, on the back cover the
    chateau.

Now everyone chews gum or diets flamboyantly, there are notes on skirts,
but on these streets Nora Charles walks no leopard, Charlie Chan does not
sniff gingerly the electric chair that was to have been his, hounds that bound
along the heath are ours, usually Labradors, and the bodies though they may clutch a dated
lottery ticket crush no flowerets delicate in their narrow season. June under the Wyoming
    stamp's a different year.

Anthology's Garland

Poetry, streaming its effects in this old anthology by the editor (Miss Monroe)
of *Poetry* Chicago—thin uprights like her or Sandburg's skyscraping buildings, few beyond
    Stein
to find that word itself poetry, but often ending with a diminuendo, as if audible inside it
the mighty crash of Merle Evans-Sousa finale favored by stump politicians, tent
preachers and those who like Ben Hecht learned journalism from highcollared editors
looking like college professors or givers of lectures on the physics of light . . . one image
"of a vortex" in Lewis's *Blast* looks suspiciously like the cone made of silk with a thread
through the point which, saturated with static electricity, pulls it through a wire loop
or else one of Mr. Yeats's gyres coming at some point as absurdly as Lombroso
or Cartesian physiology, a hymn implicit in Guthrie, anyone's history of science to all
the ones who got it wrong by following imagination where it led. Bagnold levering trucks
through the Gobi desert later worked out the physics of dunes (this after perfecting the art
of reading tire tracks in loose sand like any Sioux), here the spectacle of verse failing not
    because
not everyone's Olympic class (James Dickey's poem on the pool race I illustrated,
    preferring the one
not used of crumpled beer can) but rather, look! inside itself, not knowing really which the
classics are, Ralph Hodgson underrepresented and horrible banalities in the same type,
how learn humility from tiered Babels used to illustrate penguin *Commedias* when they're
    really
quite grand, tenement Colisea easier to draw than build but not impossible to build,
    de la Mare
on Hudson's nature writing delighted, finally, at the *presence* Rima makes, at last something
not a quality, stuffable as a goldthroated hummingbird, included by Peabody in cases with
    others,
Waterton blessing the occasion of living three days with a (three-toed) sloth.
For these, often carrying crimson and indigo soluble in cakes and cases for tinting views of
the Cordilleras, more often mighty landscape than Giant Sloth bones *in situ,* we develop
patient admiration evolved partly from their patience as if we should go downstairs,
stake out (as Darwin did) a square foot or so, describe each plant inside our twine,
    committing of course
every imaginable stupidity, but getting down these clovers (that Pound says taste, in their
    leaves, so like the flower)
and monocotyledenous grasses raveling out so untidily from an axis, in pencil, thin pen line
remembering Dürer's shovelful of dirt, crowned with its own babel of verdure, "crown,"
    "verdure."

Presorting

Lamby doth endear thee, fain we are to hear thee, bleeding like thy sicker rose,
    direct-addressing
near thee, that we've words to indicate nearness of relation or adjacence
much as these negative invasions (Mailstar producing stacks of envelopes
to band twice, attach D notice, mark first one in the tray 2MD,
short brush going up & down wets flaps) elbow, shoulder
their way in. Well, why not write "at leisure," when not working, in
that's to say an interval not given to tasks dropped on one
as if from a height? Because the lamb bethou'd as Stevens'd say's
struck through, painlessly, with a widebladed sword like something Roman,
heavy as a machete, carvable in stone.
Little lamb, present over & over, I would stick a day-glo
orange D or rubberband you, think of you as one zip
whoever made thee also addressed thee.
Dear Lamb: the Texas Department of Human Services sends you taking care of baby-to-be
flyer, el futuro bebé, See English Other Side. These things come in the mail
like poems. New management brought in thinks to replace the shifts with contract labor.
Lycidas no longer at this address. Flowers in the scholar's grave appease no shepherdess.
Chesterton imagines (in an oddly thoughtful ballad) Cervantes coming home from Lepanto
the stump where his hand was, they say, deserving gilt, imagining a basin errant
flat soup-dish like the barber's bowl to catch drawn blood inverted, worn
as a cap is, assertion by position that a thing's accustomed, familiar
as, lamb, th'art. Not sick, as thy cousin Rose is, but there is in
the kindness with which you are addressed an acknowledgment the space we occupy
is satisfactory. Water nymphs cling to your flanks like flukes
and, rubberbanded, you'd look like the Thompson sheep unshorn for years,
gray bales with feet.
The lamb is fierce in Chesterton, bathed in its wrath, fleeced leviathan
tearing up the silver bells and cockleshells.
We might fear the good, run from it, the bell for Dr. Barnardo's Ragged School still
in place in Mile End made pastoral from the canal, and it's a study, the use of
"mute" in their Romantic verse, mute mandrakes of the ground, mute pastoral
as one pretends surprise the tapestry's not audible. Personally I'm
still given to implosions, shrink at the unicorn in its fey fence, belling it
since like those horses in Homer it too is fierce, eats human flesh.
Help us to survive ourselves, teach poor children ironing and treadle sewing.
So, cries blacken walls still, the boredom even of that compressing our innocence
like iron bands around an armillary prisoner, engravings in a book on torture for the general
    reader.

"Green barbarism turning paradigm"

Can you deny the effect of Stevens here, this early Crispin
preceded by Crispine (in a long-line exercise in classical measures), his
parentheses too, according to Bates, needing closing.
His trouble really was quilts, asparagus beds, that the blanched moon
really was Blanche McCarthy, and that as he also said
the revolutionary times hadn't yet made verse exciting, a

proof of it the public sculpture, Lenin a ferret or tennisball, Marx
some silly Balzac helmet by Rodin, the beard in metal
only truly admirable in Munchausen, whose film he
would have loved for the family sheltering in the horse's torso,
not least for the reference to Napoleonic misadventure.
Perhaps revolutions do not "put all in question" at all,
merely turn us all into the streets, on display as if in a grade school
or waiters proffering to some prussian overling, for inspection, their hands
in the empty salle. He'd want our bottom porcelain taking on
the tinge implicit in the glaze, separate, inferior bonding, organisch
as if the clay hand implicate in palest pink (shepherdess rosette) whilom
we know from Fragonard garden cupids such things are gray, lit
by caput mortuum, asphaltum, touches of clay-green
a kind of opposite (like gradeschool color wheels' yellow, purple
opposed wedges) to pale rose and white of courtier-lover skin
Tussaud heads stuck or screwed into dusty blue, metallic pink
only the eye, glance, how gesture in the hands follow these restores
extremities to a common body. It may not be irrelevant, thinking on
these pastoral rentier *types* (in their way minor politicians of love)
to entertain in memory the surprise in *Marat/Sade*
when the clown's latest bucket of poured blood runs blue.
They weren't our color, as they weren't that of the stone cupids.
Say simply that. The photo'd face of Enrique Torres, "history senior," on
yesterday's *Daily Texan,* eyebrows knit with lips in a Copan sneer
may have a "right to be educated," if rights include a passive,
capons spitted turning to a common sprocket. You'd think if anything
the right is more precise to have his education matter, "his
education" then too much a property, put your degree
to work, but raucous louts like "right" in English, short, rhymes
with fight. Bile in a late teen is bile still, like any
Independent in Cromwell's army, passionately aware that when
we'd routed the ruffed and all the laws remade the truth
as there, patent, in the Bible might by some wicked oversight
be slighted still, like being dickered out of a pension.

Dinner Service Wind Chimes

flattened spoons mostly hang from cunningly tied transparent gut to
bent-out tines of a flattened fork to the four corners of a
compass rose, when the wind blows thin fairy tinging audible close to,
the butter spreader suspended from a hole through its base a
clapper to worn flat spoons, charming in itself pendant from eave
reminding me of Grimaldi's stagecraft, not only that link sausage
he'd steal from vagrant pans was apparently by his acting believ-
ably itself, themselves (more than his mouth watered) but like Grass's garbage
sculptor in *Dog Years* he'd make things into other things, coal scuttle boots
being mentioned, and what he'd do with a giant cheese, amiable on the stage
as Harpo, yet this amiable clown seems to have been no stranger to courts,
a wife-beater, possible molester of daughters. When he retired the audience's grief
appears to have been genuine, there'd been in him something of Ariel, or Dickie

as described by Charles Lamb. When you consider that cummings wrote up Savo,
Benchley the Marxes, and Beerbohm mad for Cissie Loftus (T. S. Eliot ditto)
and Gallus for Cytheris in Slavitt's elegant translation of the *Eclogues* (incorporating
    comment)
all these suitably about self-alteration (the Young Man in American Literature, theme
of initiation) as this fork, these spoons, the finish worn and pressed out of them,
brass under silver, hang in mutual accommodation not envisioned by their manufacturers
and I've seen also trans-media performances, led about by a woman with accordion
    (played well
with periodic discords) in white she was, a sand pit, votive candles, people in a riverbed,
    agile
treasure hunt, ceremonial combat on square net with tunked bowls, some hilarity, much
childishness, none of it strictly art as such or Beuysian traps for modifying "such," more duck
into fish, motives and talent flawed but as a set of things, and series one was led to
my kindness as a pack feeling, Johnsonian willingness to-be-pleased kicked in
and you're left with a souvenir still like something out of the twenties, glorious nude
against a painted drop like a borrowed kimono, retroactive talisman for what you've seen
as if this student recital, park in the dark, sparklers & flashlights, one homemade tent made
a lantern, no one strictly a performer, more like watching Punch heads being moulded than
the play itself, or first appearance of horizontally striped tights in mannered Shakespeare,
pulling us back to italic, if not indeed mud painted on thighs, what's deliberate nonverbal
    and scarcely willed.

Mistaken Identities

Intending one's intention (like reading Pound reading) tells us
too little though all's promised. Perhaps all facing mirrors do
over the long haul is dissipate energy. Paddling the river inlet near Barton Springs
(no buffalo) a snake in the water sashayed nearly, mottled brown moray,
our pup more taken by geese with red bill facings. Big turtles went
splosh off logs. We passed, leaving, the set for *Comedy of Errors,*
little pastel village. Remarkable, the utter randomness of accent, black soft r
so different in effect from British, such thumpings, rant, yet the words themselves
already a suitable instrument for tenderness (a lead black man and very blonde sister
taking little advantage of it) and female wit. They all
come into the audience for baksheesh, one Dromio routed by a Spitz with
perfect timing. The program's cruder version of the production teeshirt
spells it "seperated at birth," the humor, humors reminding me Zukofsky
labored on the meanings (even here) of eyes and I, that and
the *Ethics* framework to think labor and work into one banner, *Rudens* and a rope end,
perhaps not much end to our silliness either (master and servant
match-fading, the lovely convention of mistakability). We came to see a spectacle
like what he'd make fun of, his Theseus judging, as here the information dump, play's
    glad hand
went by default, least playing grandest but it all came right midway from the
power of this neanderthal machine driving buffalo to cliff edge, wasteful, their
eyes on the feast after (in the sky, starting low, then higher the androgynous moon).
Criticism is defeated, routed as if by a Spitz (another critic, Marianne Moore would say,
    like ant, like swan)
the basting puns laid to one side like the doll infants in the dumbshow scene.

There is an assent here, as if to rhyme or to acting often inaudible
and as it went on the play began to be able to be heard, above everyone's r's, cowardly
    runnings, till it
didn't matter, rope end, gold chain, the characters plot-dyed, sails
half-furled on spars behind the jumbled flats's vertical blue stripes
invisible in any light, not even provisional proof the set's a port, yet thinking on them,
imaginary locus of the one Antipholus's wish to be away its painful
artifice, like beware of the dog sign when there's no dog, became not request but a dead fact
like a chair, told not against us, the magic that any short person may play Ariel,
stage light through our Canadian fizzy water in wine glasses urging us
to attend this year's *Andronicus* and cheer those rubber severed wrists, the moon
still not latex, still sailing in a different sea, not better than the luminous painted one
you put up by convention in your bedroom but different and still prior.

Fits of Piqué

If "any list is complete" then, similarly, nothing is ever out of place, Hubert's
    "displacement"
of printed page, painted surface not an event even as one might standing in a parking lot
remember when it was fields. Something of that nostalgia (if there's such a thing as
    nonsentimental nostalgia)
is in Doris Cross's dictionary blowups so lovingly annihilated. In Dixie's garden, a patch
    smaller than some quilts
newspapers are spread under what are just becoming cucumbers. The effect is very odd,
    as if vegetables are reading. Doris
has up, in her kitchen, in a line above the shelves ranked Quaker Oats boxes reduced by
    muddy green
and blue acrylic to that pudgy smiling face, a word or two (often funny as something saved
    or like
descriptions as opposed to fact what's found in a small boy's pockets) and on the end
    one with
Doris's black and white catalogue face pasted on over it in flat black Taliesin quaker oats hat,
bland as the original from the mouth probably being the same width. Doris's mouth is always
the same width. She smokes, and speaks with intervals between the words. Note that this,
    put down
as a *fact,* means this poem is not addressed to Doris Cross, since it would be telling her things
she knows. I think her brutalization of blownup definitions is her making them tell her
    what she
doesn't know, the huntress with hawk on one shoulder, leopard on the other, her words all
    aquiver, the
humor this verge between hunting and forcing. Last night I wrote a poem about a
    Shakespeare
in the park play, *The Comedy of Errors,* including as almost the reason for the production
    a teeshirt
Shakespeare (in rock finery), Elvis Presley in doublet, captioned "Twins separated at
    birth?!" ho ho,
the photocopied program bearing a bad redrawing (or was it the original) the word spelled
    seperated. I've told Doris
to chuck Webster and cleave to Samuel Johnson's *Dictionary,* my place to point out
    "oats" to her in it

but doubt that even "harmless drudge" would seriously displace her allegiance unless she,
     finding harm in it
is on her very own piqued.

Ecotropic Poem

Penn Warren on the *Ancient Mariner* in *Selected Essays* making cozy fun of Mrs. Barbauld
     who
in a drawing room would have dissected him limb from limb, licks his
paws like Jerome's lion thinking he's translated the Bible into lion, picks
polite quarrels with critics then living but not, assuredly, Barbauld.
Now we do it another way, *my* Emily Dickinson, engage the text on a plain so level
it's like oh Tennyson's salt marsh indistinguishably becoming sea, this poem
this critic chimerical as form and content, "merely in the mind."
Do I bring freshwater Lake St. Clair to de la Mare's *Desert Islands,* do readers
of Hakluyt explore? One evolves a taste for Darwin's style. Yet these—I was reading
Carolyn Kemp's monograph on the Dickinsonian nay, noticed Anderson's *Stairway of*
     Surprise not present
in the notes, no Gelpi, Whicher (no quote in Gelpi which is *not* in Whicher, odd doubling)
     and
can't help ask if we're beyond, so, those kinds of reading that these are Trobriand, primitive
despots of departments, heads.
What we're invited to share isn't all; late Kwakiutl couldn't burn it fast enough, "plight"
no longer comic. Imagine salmon are styrofoam, that moves nothing, on a large scale waste
is not a question of conscience, not the result of an attitude. Pretend
you're an inspector of earths, come to some place with leis draped over herms, ask
why (what?) all those shells aren't being used to pave roads. Roads you find are a function
of a hundred desires, like the man you interrogate's feather robe. No one said it was easy.
Ordure's a leather unguent. Anyone can talk about a snake head with squash teeth as
emblematic, more than striking, full of a meaning that hushes, not Sousa.
We aren't buddhist, underwater, opening our eyes looking at a trout, in that poem
by Gary Snyder. This notion that saying is saying falls down. If Dickinson's
poems were letters to Elizabeth Barrett should they've been charged double postage? Define
address, define address. Aim this at some notion of bamboo serenity
and it comes back upholstered (quite properly) in red crepe, dusty rose.
Design is like intent to make a chair "like a toy truck" (Stumpf), thing executives
who make decisions you dislike sit in, sit in. There are words
in general, Hamlet's "Words, words, words" and "Ponder my words," particulate
as photons charging from the sun intent on mischief. These overlords have shoulders like
     pagoda eaves.
Engage them on questions of style, and be prepared to lose. Realms depend
on the executive ashtray, silvered without, cherry red within, oblong, crenelated.
Falstaff in solitary has only the voice we imagine for him, you want them to bug you.
The tail end of an outworn mode, the underground magazine its own cartoon of itself,
habitués of healthfood stores so often the beginning-to-age, that are taggable.
I think exactly what you imagine will save the world from a habit of holistic thinking.
Visualize world peace (imagine religious whales), this bamboo tea strainer
biologically correct. Go dig in your back garden, under the tree (tomato plant), you will find
a square iron box you lift free of the dirt with a large iron ring
there in the top. The key to open it is your house key.

The Black Potholder

wasn't real to me, a kitchen shadow, till I lifted with it the metal teapot
(Assam and Lipton) and it was like grabbing some funeral pall, heavy velveteen
so what besides tea has died here and the red and yellow electric company holders, so
much smaller, less adequate on top as a kind of mushroom tea cozy, elfcapped stainless steel
vulgarized slightly by the contact. Beyond conjunction of texture is this non-area, substances
        become thought,
their ideas compared in collocation like a drunk's sentence, a beauty like Harlen
sitting in his antique dentist's chair, so much a statement about the hopes rather
than the pretensions of science, black clothing against its drugstore blender cream and green
in the memory, which imagines for it leather straps or the shot of Kosta elegant and unclad
pouring this hatted sunglassed Bad Spy coffee from an urn (too large you'd think to serve
        to proffered cup)
and you wonder why, after Puritan sumptuary laws we did it again, went black so doggedly
F. X. Tolbert and Ann's shifting whites and blacks a pleasure, the domino death wears
        white. I used
to wear Goodwill black suits with purple shirts, and have a photo of Kim Reale in
        rhinestoned red on the Pepsi rink
in '84, me managing, black suit, red shirt.
Ruined a pair of black shoes fetching the (white sailorsuited) chimp's hurdles off white ice
        that year
and I've poured myself utterly rich tea, what you might call black tea, to my favorite stark
        white mug with the
pencilmark dings inside near the handle where glaze failed, little marks as if incised in clay
a pleasure, the pot heavy with tea, in black so temporarily, held "in" black so I think of sitting
across from Doris Cross going through her Webster for words it'd be neat for her to,
        photocopied, alter with paint
and ink's collective deletion till what's *really* said, definitional remarks become statement
shines out, as the Quedlinburg Gospel's *Quoniam* in gold, signed by Samuhel (perhaps
        addressed by Raban Maur,
says the *Times*), celebritous medievaldom facing a scribe dipping (is it) his pen into a pot of
gold ink on a turned stand perhaps thirty-two inches high, over his right shoulder a winged
        bull reading
what, on the painted pages, it or he, monstrous angel, might be said to know's written on the
        facing page
and so on, in near-uncial script, legible as my tea is potable, pot under what might be black
        figured satin
with square envelope on top for the paten, of the same material, chasuble ditto over white alb.

NEA Poem

It wasn't that in 1985 I was ruining my eyes with fine print
cassette titles shelved sideways in a record store, or reseating
my toilet with plastic wood and plaster on rotten flooring up which
slugs, attracted by the sawdust, would sometimes come, teetering
over the lip of the bowl, or the long walk Sundays to the temporariest of jobs—
all these I believe were under my control, fact chosen like a tired rhyme
in an anthology by Jessie Rittenhouse (her second Modern Verse
one yesterday in Goodwill looking very new) or Helen Vendler,

whom I've always liked for her little book of Stevens lectures,
inheriting (the clipping says) Bate's chair at Harvard this July,
first woman who etc., these no more important than the glamor
properly invested in Ginsberg, Corso, Orlovsky, there in '58
to sell the banned *Big Table* in Grolier and Pangloss,
their presence salvific as if Whitman came to lecture but that
the twenty-six years between those dates I spent learning to write verse
tumbled me like something in a drum, lump in a New Age basket, rose quartz or jasper,
non carborundum garnet opposed to bloodstone I find Tristan's ring was made of,
industrial versus anything impractical (though those going up against Tristram
knew he'd hang 'em on a tree) so it's as if, in any period here, Wallace
Stevens wearing straw hats in New York, of two minds about law school,
to now it's some medieval-lay atmosphere encapsulated in, polished by,
the clarity of lay with its cool curses. When I applied to edit for the Texas Bar
they solved the conflict between their publications and mine by agreeing,
a bit wolfishly I thought, to describe verse as my hobby.
In Boston Little, Brown lost hundreds of my drawings without apology,
no limit to what we take. So government acknowledgement, even with
no money attached, soothes battered and abraded souls, soothed mine in '85.
I bought clothes in London (though I retain to this day a habit
of looking in on Goodwill), saw there and in Paris Manets, Tissots and others
I'd ached to see light glance off the surface of, absorbed through my surfaces
buildings, tricks of diction, recorded "Mind the gap" in Bank Street, places
Eliot and Dickens walked, stood, Gladstone and Newman still doing so in Tussaud's,
and it was good for me, took off the horror of my working life. I had
cross-checks on half my subjects from one green government one in the mail,
like a tax refund in its buff envelope, and what are these legislators
rousing Art Fear in lonely voters, that which ran Garland, Sandburg, even Hecht
to Chicago to write for the *Sun* when Stevens thought Santayana thought
doing to take from us so little, raise even the question of their right
to judge what they think requires no expertise to make, returning
the nineties to the teens, straw hats, Darrow, makers of art the monkeys
in fundamentalism's replayed trial, the funeral parlor vivid yet on palmleaf fans.

Outside Grenoble

where the howling dogs's hackles smoothed to mewling, the graveyard all dead vines,
matted tracings, bound together stone not much older than the nineteenth century, but
from architectural morosity seeming much older, say a park belonging to de Sade's father,
as Montaigne's round tower spoke medieval in a late idiom, second Yquem,
and it's nothing, not at night, to imagine some raw February, the graybrown of the vines
repeating sky's overcast, that something in trailing cloth might have come
from a tomb, perhaps, perhaps a tomb, or else the caretaker's daughter, caught up
in the atmosphere contrived for her by father's occupation (so tied to its setting) and
innate good taste of one with too little to do, might carry a Bronte volume, Bell's poems
with wonderful Heep preface, in the not uncomely hand marked with a delta
of silk, not black but pigeon-gray darker in light fading like a compliment
in speech that matched her hats, this exhalation of a taste for matching one's milieu
is too easily imagined acting on the dogs as depressant, dismal inhibitor, this
trick of talking of states in terms of drugs, murk become Merck, likewise characteristic, as if

rhyme floating free of troubadour taste retained a touch of blackened kitchen,
memory a kind of habit as Butler used to say for whom Italy was specific to his drizzle,
the genre's ineluctably woven in as by Shalott, wholly the effect of gleam—a hard
thing or glimpsed leyline pool—in softer medium, yarny thread, the fascination
of Tristram's armor wearable like an undergarment, the plastic tank, texture in
another's terms, nothing like Basil's "Throwing the Moon" in which I suppose
action becomes gesture but still believable (in his players' pastel stone), the way
Seurat's unimaginable embankments alter the value of rooms or Frankenthaler's
    landscapes won't
impose themselves on classical conventions replacing remembered paint by paint,
similarly not knowing bodies or game rules we recognize, come to impose on Basil's players
the blankness with which we front people dressed for a role, who in real spectatorial time
(not "ours" because shared) act the way they're to act, as chess pieces in photographed ads
are examples of deportment for which the memory of rules fades, deliberately, like
cigarette butts enlarged beyond their function even as discards.
Have we "shifted," discussing this, from the graveyard in Corot bankside gray-browns
unrelieved in the caretaker's daughter's costume (her face transparent as oatmeal)
as if described locale, at best sketched in, in spite of the pretense
it's situate in Michelin, or is it permitted to remark that the feel of a milieu
may be desirable as Gibbings' Seine, Pope-Hennessy's Provence, our pleasure in aspect
an aspect of our pleasure in anything, that glasses exist for wine, brushes for paint,
that we can be merely in some relation to color, as crossing any field
reminds us even pleasurably that terror is possible, even imminent.

Poetry's Disruptive Force

The black candle saved for years burned days back to the socket, kind of a
charcoal pool not bright like most candlewax on brass, more grit
like the dust in the back of your glass-tube radio, even the light shed
less somehow than foresty greens, wax reds, blues our mugs repeat,
a domestic spell, like watching milk curdle, and it's not for nothing we
put off helplessness, politeness of not looking at to memorize people on the subway,
kindness of our wearing clothes. The parakeet feathers sit in a bowl unused for anything.
Milk we pour in tea, our meal meal-colored, not blue. If you throw a stone
that's polished and clear it produces clarity, lines you "draw" on the table
after the throw indicated in air, not something embroidered on a formal cloth,
real grid like crossed swords danced among. The stones's resolutions
of their vectors, center of gravity in a ship drawing, permisslble arc from the keel
help determine axes, rather like a frame, external, square, pulled through
one of its points; the stones in a plane *are* the field. Verse is like this,
poetree, on the back of a leather jacket in Dickey's poem, epater les barbiers
by means of lifting bellies and lift, the first light. Gregory Beene says
of poetry in *lift 3* can it destroy things? probably not. In this he is
mistaken. The potlike shape of your cat like a bad ceramic or fake
rock you stick the key in to hide it, iconic representation of the rolled-open
sardine tin (I once painted one all in yellows Jim Haining has) a
grotesque imitation of the passive, that possession is "defensive"
yet another grammatical remark. Spectroscopic analysis of the cat
reveals . . . amethysts and coralest pinks, live apple yellows and blues
fading to rose, all done in curves like a punk's stiffened hair combed

toward each other, say esses roughly converging toward a mussed peak,
that we saw on the way to San Antonio framed by perfectly ordinary
clouds before, behind, a rainbow made of fur probably (I thought) ice
crystals so disposed for what reasons by some wind but there
in the midst of vivid gray clouds with white highlights, this patent apocalypse
was in part a remark spinning off from the spell my candle
had it burned all night in a greenhouse, visibly, would have been
part of even with the louvers closed, the textural imposition
common to both identical if, having imagined green plants and panes
I then imagined the car trip as some mother-ship revelation on the
neighbor coast, though it was three p.m., outside Seguin.

Behoving the Troove

The pc crowd still wears washable plaid shirts like the ones
at MIT living on vended crackers awaiting complication. The look behind
their glasses is expectance. I worked in their science museum shop, vending
computer chip tie clips, Time = Money teeshirts (heavy and clothy, feeling moist,
smelling of laundry from being stacked on shelves, the Charles adjacent
where years before at Harvard I feathered under parabolic bridges, liked
color (any color) in the dim streets and still have a slide of some
paint cans, one brilliant orange, brighter than underhull paint
in a *Crimson* trash can, bought ceramic bright-blue beads at Marimekko while
at MIT they played with fractals now on screens in offices
like fish if not sliding by, and Ai's wee workshop signs in Grolier meant
farther down the street, quite properly, Artificial Intelligence.
It's easy to argue we're in the wrong trade, missed out from
thinking cracker crumbs on shirts looked bad, my friends into
music and heroin, becoming a concern with self the anniversary reports report
some of the philosophers nearly something, Burkholder in Omaha, Corson in France
Kripke at Harvard losing himself in (oddly) reference, and only C. P. Snow
to tell us in what seemed faltering accents that after all we both use pencils.
I had to ask students, teaching schemata, how we know "pencil"
applies to little stubbies, German silver gift ones (graduation; one Brooklyn
teacher wore graph-paper shirts and a sliderule tie clip), the big
mockup hanging in Bob Slate, Stationers' window on Mass Ave, and it now
seems natural to have intuited while avoiding the formulation that
the light on my Bic in Au Bon Pain is different from how it hits
the programmer's pencil at the next table, his *Globe* somehow neater
than mine, clothier, like giftshop teeshirts, and it is nearly possible to envy
him offing to the concerts, owning like some punk of intellect the streets
still my poems are, as Woody Guthrie'd say, my dirty overalls, that
I fight in, find them comfortable, solutions Valéry would say to problems
no one would otherwise think up. It won't work, the Spencer Tracy slamming Darwin
and the Bible together in *Inherit the Wind.* Darwin's prose inherits Mark, the one
who runs naked away, beetles spilling from his mouth.

Female Goddesses

Our local women's shop (incense, teeshirts, books, fey instruments)'s composition stone
goddesses in reproduction—perhaps hard to tell sometimes from neolithic dolls, sample
　　　　ware—
are flat (Cycladic) and round (Germanic), the one like plates, the other bobbins,
both associations "female" enough, what Milton would write "femal," for anyone
assenting to the shop at all. "Very well," you say, "this is a shop." Your finger on the stone
perceives partly mastic warmer than the mere pressure of particles. In the school
I now teach at nose rings are not allowed, part for the whole, mutilation a part
of the statement. Those cave walls Eshleman lectures on bell out to make
the stomach of a goddess roughly carved and tinted, and was this felt
as digging, thing carved out, or thing carved into, language going on.
The bat squeaks or minotaur, hobbling about on two legs. Young women talk to each other
in a different tone which left to itself becomes the shop, sororal ease. We buy
Bulgarian Rose to burn, a velvet bag squat as artichoke hearts with tiny
inside pockets for stones or other charms, eight dollars, cards to mail.
The shape of going on narrative makes so hard to isolate in Conan Doyle
or Fleming still is felt. In school we have an arm with hand attached to tuck
in ceiling tile to hang down stalactish, cigarette lighter in its loose fist. Men need
no reminding they were once as gods; women seem to think imaginary polities
"were once" (taletelling part of the feminine) less warlike, Dogon doors
so much essence of cupboard presumably unlatched, your kouros Keres.
Jungian models, thinking vs. imagination, hopelessly inept here to indicate, predict
what adz on door might do, repeating ribs a locust in imagination out,
flail my key or fly tassel symbolizing rule all woven like Hurrian print invading robes,
the bull's feet clashing with his wings, horned mitre, purse. Give to stone
in expensive simulacrum its due, pay Chileans not to make more masks but goddesses
from any place to export here, invent your own, the holes with slots
like buttons nickels turn, the plugs in children's banks, wee fussies a habit of
manipulating by finger shrines for us, the moon a goddess too (though there are
countries here and there reversing sun and moon, Our Mr. Capra's), cat awaiting owl.
Your tabbiness indents a couch, this yarn your prey. Forgive the hammered
cups with frogs (male and female) notorious for spawn, these clarities
what French grown conscious of itself might do to prove a gender.
Theseus popped in a knitting bag reduced to fetish like nail or hair
which flexible as potentially lengthy might aware
of trappedness invent a cave imagining a route from it
thinks itself, himself as a thing emergent errs, subsumption no form cut in space.

Campion Crown'd

The wood salad bowls are a cliché, as are in a sense pets which are dogs
your hot sauce recipe in another sense an improvement in our lives
like the look, smell, feel of your book so new it reeks of cilantro
but the wooden bowls, carved or hollowed out of wood (irregular, not turned),
occupation for some village—I found in a yard sale, some cracked
I didn't buy, just these unflawed but certainly much used, washed, eaten from
simply in no sense immaculate, like old slippers, thing from the next village's cobbler
and you who can talk of Jerez, monkeys swinging their way from Africa

right across Spain, primeval forest gone in seconds with its niches
suffer for—what? the plants that find themselves fractionated out up the sides
of mountains, waiting for the zone shift that some day etc., well or say
the antique-type nineteenth-century Shakespeare page that finding in the
pages of Jim Haining's *Salt Lick* I laminated, photocopied, taught my class
how like this is to the meaning of singing Latin you with your relation to the English martyr
who suffered for so doing so I wondered are you related to the wild flower as well
and so got it wrong again, a rose you said (once used to crown athletic champions)
a lychnis subset coronaria, saxifrage to your book's Palenque ball-court stones, what we
know too well splitting what we don't, the dog jumping on my lap midsentence
as one wonders walking them what's that in their mouths, found in the street
invasion of thinking, what might be thought of as thought by an irrelevance, cilantro in
the windowsill, my students telling me there is an ad (the hot sauce from New York),
    bumpkin
aficionados dubious. A mind may flit like Puck, "Frankly I'm dubious" applicable for its
vaudeville dutch reply, "Pleased to meet you Mr. Dubious"'s handshake coatsleeve
    nearly covering the hand
from the period when mothers, having a bolt of yellow cloth, made suits the son would have
    to wear, Jim taking
from a life of Mencken only that he wore, a time, yellow shoes. I don't mean to push the
    silliness of knowing
irrelevants but that your name for us including martyr and flower only gradually (ballooning
    out)
extends to cover more or less your body and your book, attar of your discourse reduced to
    print.

Two Diaries

It would be like reading Greek, clarity encased in its consonants, her
decisions of that sort embedding what houseparty guests had said, then going for the
composition of them, deco sanded-glass fleurets out of time, in another frame, decoration
    become decoration,
so many peonies unlikely to read one, another Vanessa cover cruder, less like Beerbohm than
one could imagine. You think of it, Virginia in "drapery" rather than a dress, hung slat
to her being, Lady Colefax or Dame Edith in unexpected brocade, silver flowers on blue,
    and it's
the dog that intruding falls through a ship's canvas startled, unhurt, and wine at the rich's table
a bit of a bribe. Oh! the placing a word just here, Town Council inscribed on brick,
Sidney or L.'s committee meetings eluct brown surety of mind, L.'s hands (trembling) peeling
an apple, light through any back passage window summer light.
My days aren't like yours in any particular beyond a smudged blue bowl given us by Carol
    Wright
under (as cold-type r shoulders under cap T) the blue Maine shade bought to match writing on
Barbara and Edward's oat lamp, her decorous speech nervous as she knew *Ulysses*
    flummoxed
partway through *Dalloway* and look, her life's mothy syllables the dust on them, iridescent as
Vanessa's gobs so in reproduction too like Bonnard (or la John) to matter for us as is
the word iridescent, dead end in literature we won't be reminded of barring *Lamia,*
pure balance of philosopher's gaze (Foucault's) on prismatisms, gone for a day to sylvan
    boles, the

eighteenth century, beloved of Lang, breathed on by Boucher, and yet (as she says) and yet
elastic membrane between Evelyn and fact, the writing sifts like pollen to the forest floor,
    thing
to analyze eons later on the breast of Palestinian hoard, you have to keep a love of London
through its narrow aperture of affordable solidity, tuft spared by mower's bombs
and when it doesn't buck you up enough, vocational avidities, you fill
pockets with stones and die, thinking for decor of Ophelia and for truth of stones.

Fabula Rasa

I was talking to Holly about gifts and Christmas and decided
our pets are better to give gifts to even than friends or parents. Why?
she wanted to know, a bit pugnaciously, full of presents for Zach and others,
quite a long list. The necklaces she makes for people suit them, as the lobster earrings
Yvette bought her suit her. So I was thinking of the suitable, and what Octavio
Paz says Lévi-Strauss made of gift-giving, a whole system in anthropology and
today over lunch saw a gift of blood book, about its donation (with statistics)
in England and elsewhere, and what it means. So these were in my mind
like the light moulded figures, pale purple donkeys and such, in a creche, manger
two little Xes, the straw not straw rather like the flat yarn we used to weave potholders of,
the *taking* of a risk, a chance, a gift. It's sure that being given
a gift puts one in danger, the necklace with its painted wooden cross redefining the wearer
not as Christian maybe but of a coloring, the sort of person who might wear
dull reddish lobsters pendant from the ear, these animals in the creche
beginning to move a little, ease to the ribcage from a shift in weight. You go
a year without thinking of their kneeling Christmas Eve, not legend so much as
    acknowledgment
that you've adjacent stables, midden, pattern established way back in the Danube valley,
rather like an innyard—place for animals, central steaming mound, people here,
Rabelais and Chaucer's cock, Bremen musicians feeding right into Gunter Grass, no
more meant by this than, as the Czar's ballet children wore lyre insignia we're all born
under the sign of the stable, it's our star. So why the gift to animals, knit cap for dog,
catnip mouse with a bit of holly on given our smoke-black cat named Cobweb, what's
the myth we act on giving presents to those known as presences, their names ours,
    ineluctably
generic as brandy or whisky chained to a decanter like a collar . . . why give
the animal a thing felt as appropriate, which won't define the beast any more than Cobweb
    or Phoebe,
present not itself named, not "bone" to it but that it, looking at it from a Santa cap is
as we know generous, given to giving its presence to us, the gift of making sounds
signifying we should feed it, but not words. We talk to them, our words companionship
or trained monition but never simply speech, the ribbed and ribald throwaway as when we say
socks are clocked, the bend in the road endured by it, arriving as we arrive at relatives'
so new for the animals, something baptismal like a Latin root, ex- for out of the car, off
we say, to keep "down" a separate command, and in apology for these, the multifarious
    prohibitions
and durational existence under couches, the animal flat midafternoon, heaped like
language in a basket we give them something, mouse doll to kill, a squeaky red-orange lion,
things not imaginable as toys, more like the hen's china egg, some model appanage
because they're dumb, don't speak, so a thing we give them is more like themselves,

impersonating gift, standing or kneeling in place as the animals' presentment of themselves
to us, to then some dignity like the red circles looking like felt on the cheek
of the man I saw today dressed as a toy soldier, the round patches an acknowledgment
of paint and placement, some rationale of scale and materials violently overcome as it is true
if you creep late Christmas Eve to your little creche the moulded animals, stupidly obedient,
   likewise kneel.

To a Ghost Rose

perhaps the one named after lace—in any case probably a white one,
pink at best, Disney correct to imagine brighter reds poured on, nodding
globes in the Pittsburgh ad, the tinct veneer. I say, says Mallarmé,
and you're right to have got "a flower," at least a fleuret, beginning cluster,
like the dimity things in yellow, blush orange, the quilts of mixed petal
returning by green leaf to Goethe's magnifier's marcasite or tortoiseshell handle,
perfect for looking at glass roses.
"The very attar of the rose," says Merrill, is Time. One subsection
of how to go on is getting over flat statement. Olson's good at it.
The body one might have been's a rose, transparent as any ghost
or Beerbohm young self buttonholing eld. You live long enough,
you grow right through your body. My grandfather in his last year,
leg cut off at the knee, was so fine, his white hair, the Polish bones
of his face, if I read anywhere "transparent" of a face I think of him,
beautifully fragile. There were in Purgatory transparent souls for other reasons,
not much in any case for casting shadows, even as smoke does, unearthly
for a body to transmit light, like the little fish not much more than
eyespeck and a backbone. Our culture probably never got over glass, a pun
to have liquid in it and ice. I wrote once about encasing a diamond
in lucite and then increasing the plastic's hardness index—till, presumably,
facets cease to function. This could be fame, immortality, a footnote
to Stevens, saltcellar among the goblets. Daily attars include us
in their plans, rather as perfumes cling for centuries to a stoppered bottle,
the aroma a historical inhalant. Where was I at twenty-one? not where
is that waif now, what's gone was always gone, and so you send me to these
Merrill poems called "Divine" on the cover—they hadn't *Elements* secondhand.
A reader's tinted Ephraim on the fore-edge orange, enough sound there,
like Euphrates on the biscuit. We take our roses on trust.
I did a stretch, not quite a year, with Nature's Jewelry which gilded
roseleaves for pendants, earrings, not to mention laurel and parsley,
an education to see light on a velvety leaf, the pores stopped with gold.
It may be why, that same odd shift of light, mummy cases
apply the painted eye and eyebrow over it, as if gold is part
somehow of recollection. The mirrors the mother of the Muses looked in
were, after all bronze. Some haruspex may have wanted to gild
feathers or a bird skull, just to look at, carry in a bag or flat
in a book, two boards shaved thin, recessed as if for wax.
It's a light business, this ghost stuff, the ectoplasm in Boston
increasingly vulgar, eventually bladder hands and fingerprints
but at first a pretty notion, that we'd exude some gaseous
semisolid, nothing like electric rays of snipped-off leaves but

the body itself thinned, issuing some notion of itself as proof
a solid thing is its idea, only later photographed or cast in wax,
more like Donne going to sleep in his shroud, as roses
to our eye are always to some extent their leaves.

Playing Santa Claus

What it was like if you don't lie (and Santa probably doesn't lie) was
a lumpish plastic bag's red pullover jacket edged with white, wide
trousers with drawstring, triangular red hat with white pompom, pullover
vinyl boot tops with white fur, a brand-new Dynel beard and wig so
flourishing the whole head could vanish in them and a belt
repaired twice, the tang a bit short for safety. I folded the boot tops
in around themselves to stick inside Jim Haining's black western boots, the
fur trim overlapping, sewed a small rent under one armhole and spent
the night before trimming my bangs from underneath to see out of
and the walrus moustache, total-war cascade over the gauze mouth-hole so
I could talk from under it (breathless from a cold and pills I'd not say much)
and used spare hair, of a brightness only nylon can achieve, for eyebrows
just to try clear rubber glue on bandaid, a bust of an idea, had to
go the day to a costume shop for a better belt, charging also rectangular
spectacles I thought a good idea for definition, brought curved cuticle scissors
to snip the beard's too loose elastic for a tighter tie, an olive drab long training
leash to tie the one down pillow to my front, a small tinsnips just in case
and white cotton Kodak gloves. That day I wore my red suit anyway
I used on circuses, white shirt and broad red tie and best black shoes (people'd
pass me and say "Turn it down!") recruiting 7th graders and Eve (8th) who wore last night's
long red dress and red stockings for elves, green felt caps ending in a bell,
for a better entrance and distribution of gifts around the tree I helped hang earlier
with red and green stockings. The school office hall door has a full-length mirror.
Julio helps decide how to strap on the pillow. I put on trousers over my red trousers,
tie the drawstrings, stick redstockinged feet in boots through the vinyl liner, settle top fur.
It's easy then to get the top on, pat it around the pillow, add the belt (what height
for best effect?) A flap of belt hangs loose as I knew it would
and I ask has anyone a black paperclip. No, so I take the one sleighbell on a loop
of green cord from lost and found, loop it over the belt and through itself to jingle
and keep the belt shut, tie on the beard with care, elastics over the ears,
add wig and settle hat. Very little me is visible. I try the glasses,
rebending them to peer over at the letter I'll bring in, saying
"Is this Kirby Hall?" (It works. Many children say it is.) And for
a while practice the walk, breathing deeply, feet splayed a little,
back straight. It's surprising how many things you think to do with gloved hands
make a bad angle. Akimbo is good, and hands just meeting over mighty stomach.
Ho ho and Mer-r-ry as a whisper, jingling the bell. Eight-minute call.
My elves collect. We're on, bursting in from the back, so teachers, kindergarteners,
lower school generally turns, moves into the aisle so we move through and in them,
I'm embraced by one (nearly knee level), shake hands with others delicately, gloved.
The spectacles tend to fall off if I look down. We pass out gifts. I sit, am photographed.
The hubbub is controlled. We do quite well. One elf, mischievously, hands me a present
marked Mr. Burns. I say I'll get it to him, her smile conspiratorial.

The head's present's gone, from under the tree, and I worry about that
while praising, sorting, greeting. All play with presents. Teachers beam, our exit
low-key, a middling rapid progress, back to (I say) the office for our milk and cookies.
To be a mythic being is as their minds—I could have played it in a paper beard,
I say, the prettiness of how in their minds it is without, it seems, suspicion
(I get called Santa Claus anyway for the red suit), and taking off the garments,
hanging wig and beard to cool, the pillow debelayed, boot tops, belt and spectacles in bag,
separating theirs and mine did not feel like circus or backstage conjuring (we ended a Dallas
public video taking clown makeup off to credits rolling), rather a thin, high emotion than
     fatigue
perhaps Renault's *Mask of Apollo,* aftermath of mimicking a god, and I confess
having made a quiet prayer to Saint Nicholas before going on, that kind of thing.

L. S. Lowry, Christmas Day

Thinking of Lowry's life, evangelically raised, can it have been what he wanted, those
pictures of factories *on* streets, hugely approachable by walking, behind them churches,
     factories
behind those, people a litter in front, foregrounded as if the buildings are their furniture.
     One day he
met Ford Madox Brown (who painted *Work*) doing the Manchester murals, mercantile
     history
in colors suitable for unicorns, faded rose, gold, whites. To stump Midland streets finding
a bank facade dancing in the wind, your heart leaps up to it, the threadbare classes
with daughters now angels of the lord, the city touched by coal as auto, tire manufactury
colored my Detroit, black and yellow buildings like yellow pages ads for plating of all kinds,
the little shops that pressed out tail lights for mammoth vehicles, jewels of red plastic's
beaded-area diffusers like the giant ruby you could buy for your bike's back fender ending in
flattest circle, stiff bolt through the middle, nut. You'd find condensers in the street, bit of
wire in alleys with flattened copper ends, nickel-ended fuses sifted into gravel like a mandible
and say the animals of which they're parts must be romantic too, terrapins ten feet
long, their bones in cliffs, coral-island cars around the plants at River Rouge, even
     Ashmolean
of our own, whole shops under glass at Greenfield Village, only surprising a gray
lethargy suppressing, like the grime, white thought though downtown buildings
are medieval, patinate. It's the simultaneous extinguishment of promise you paint.
Our murals too incorporate mollusca, though mostly goggled people by furnaces,
engines like carcasses from hooks, moving, to which our workers (and supervisors)
adopt stances they think appropriate—alert, whether caring or nonchalant it's clear
they understand, the factory only a big machine like a bicycle to which one might attach a
     motor.
And this is where we live, these houses, tract but not like spinners' cement stucco with
     green windows
on streets designed to turn the impact of iron wheels. Collieries are often coastal; you can
     see the sea.
From ours you saw a great lake, clay-green going metallic gray, sooty as overcast, only blue
on clearest mornings, and here the Fords built a manor with one magnificent Cézanne
(watercolor on paper tea service) in a front room taking that light as it came
and we'd painters enough, our light green as copper, clear as Paris just not
that dusty lemon so good falling on gardens and women. We could like

Sickert have done more (than we did) with artificial light, buses in front of the Bonstell,
J. L. Hudson Christmas windows to compare, galoshed, with Crowley's, toes cold
from slush seepage or bitter cold snow powdery, twilight sky as if absorbing light
but you wouldn't have had for our people the same feeling, that one late one
of you lit so harshly in the kitchen, your face taking light like the empty dishes,
everything mostly shadow, falling to shadow no matter what, whatever you do
so you sit there for the photographer to finish and go away, Christmas
what it was a hundred years or so before for Engels, unintelligible as a pig
or atrocious hat toward which you feel warmth, these huddles of solitaries
each with a history, like Manchester's, you paint by painting what it looks like now.

Reliquaria

How very very nice it is to see beneath a quote from Elizabeth Barrett's
Casa Guidi Windows that they "are in dire need" of repair
in a newsletter from the Friends of the Browning house there,
O bella libertà, O bella! so much as her verse often is
like a letter from her. "Nearly $6,000 was contributed to our
1989 appeal." Another grant to duplicate the chandelier leaves free
reproducing another piece of furniture in that painting. I've seen
Dickens's razors in a scuffed green velvet case (and a desk and chair
very like his at Tussaud's, with him sitting there), there's Mark
Twain's pipe in Hannibal and the pool table of course, nearly nothing
of Poe's, and in Austin we've Gertrude Stein's cloak, but in general
when the poet vanishes . . . whatever happened to Gerard Manley
Hopkins's chalice? How many swords owned Stevenson?
Housman's porridge bowl would be desirable (Yale has
Johnson's teapot, and I still remember William Alfred saying at Harvard
he'd seen the cups and they're *tiny,* "all those stories of his putting away cups and cups!")
so it's not nothing. Jim Haining (who reports on Twain's pipe) has
a poem about the little objects, knives and things, you use a while
and then they go away. It matters to our imaginations that poets are surrounded
by environs, artifacts, an eye patch for Joyce, Pound's handmade table (still being
used, Kenner asserts, years later in the Paris apartment), somehow mattering, the
portrait by Hazlitt, Baudelaire's sketch of Jeanne, Manet's lapel ribbon
would be wonderful, and then the houses, Dove Cottage like a playhouse
for Alice (judging from photos), fey plastered ingles, somewhere Wordsworth's tatty books
rested, what catalogues call "shaken" bindings, no matter when you consider their trips
in pockets, Keats's Chaucer travell'd, Burns's tombstone so much a writing desk,
Lewis Carroll's meditatively beautiful camera lens an extension of his face
oh fugitive! like orange pips shook from an envelope. These are
the furniture of moments like the rosewood wands I got in Flosso's shop
Houdini may have touched—partly coming near the bodies of illustrious Edwardians,
an exhibit of their cat bowls . . . Turner's travel kit (made from a leatherbound
book ripped back to the cover)'s lumps of watercolor in shapes like Lot's wife,
half melted, still *usable* if he'd come back, Thoreau's handmade lead pencil
stuck through a card by a pencil drawing of Walden sounded, we've these
haphazard surveyables. Someone must still bake in Plath's oven. No one
knows Villon's whereabouts. You want a great age, like Tennyson's,
outliving reputations, a world of objects that were patently your favorites.

So in spite of Beerbohm's funny drawings and the late Browning's dining habits
(Carlyle liked feeding him, cherished it) a house in Italy that sheltered Shelley
and Byron's worth keeping up even with the dark green walls its
bookmark indicates, along with a teardrop diamond in a heartshaped setting
of smaller diamonds with, above, very nearly unaccountably, two more flanking
what seems a crown, enameled if that isn't an odd reflection off
a central diamond but in any case a teardrop made a heart then coronée
that was, they say, her engagement ring, the shank thin, probably large
enough to go on over a glove but it's sunk into the velvet or felt
fold and is of course enlarged so one can't be sure.

Dark Linguists

You could write (quite easily) a poem in a language you don't know. It's
done all the time. Here you break a too conventional association—you're
writing in lines, that kind of poem—and here the precise word, epithet, for the
color of wrinkled skin on the elephantlike elephant we imagine we're less
familiar with than Africa's—once in Detroit an elephant in a local circus
picked up a pickup hand, threw him down (its foot hurt), the owner thinking
to get out of the business. Just another roustabout. There was a
room for clowns to dress in, drabness of green walls emitting tramps, what's
alien, nothing foreign to minds accepting physics, the child's interest in
Elephant Man, grotesque aberration one might easily have been, split
planarian, the crossed mock eyes of tiny roach, liver fluke, maggot
things left to themselves like someone repairing your television, activity privileged
by your dislike for it, unwillingness to reveal how bored you are.
It would be a problem, writing a line or two (would they have "sentences"?)
but length would heap, like Longleat House's handpainted Chinese wallpaper,
parroquets with tubular bamboo and something like a dove, the
best of it squiggles at the end of a climbing pink flower, not a
design to butt against a repeat. You could press on, pages of passionate gibberish,
pounding the table, groaning, however convince them or utter (well, you
know by analogy these words too make sounds) or some complexity in German
or Eskimo, strung sentence-word, or else (oh trumpet vine) a
meaning never stated, something like what the cellos only imagine when they play
winding till it hits some imperfection in your surface, or seed ingested sprouting
unwanted like wasps's young, so easy to be invaded by signs in a foreign street,
even subtitles in odd scripts under films in English, and go listening to the
sound of lace curtains like Wyeth's mind in a half-open window, fitful, uncertain.
It's all contagion, just when you've invented the animal to find it's so, my class
spent twenty minutes designing a room for people with no chairs, the paintings tall
        verticals
for standing/sitting till we noticed it was just Japan. We gnash our teeth
in imitation of the mastodon, embark on an essay and it's a water hole, go
in any case around, this stone I found, the edges sharp in scallops, folded
on one side like a troubled kidney, but usable, could it once
have been a scraper, am I obliged to imagine a tongue untaught by Hegel,
thinking its hum is like the sound of grass, some Whitman or Gary Snyder imagining
that primordial is so like what's there it is? algebra of beaded pattern,
that small bored things are flexible as scales, what counts as news different
for us who know that anything you say is speech.

Reporting Arab Wars

When Rather asks to put a thing in perspective he means give us an object
of attention, thing to focus on, so Syrians are the "key" because they are
of no importance—to what? To the "equation," defined as that which gets
"infinitely more complex" if the Israelis (struck by Scuds) choose to retaliate.
Meanwhile (Dan) Jennings on another channel talks right through a foreign newsman's
        question
to tell us it's an, um, press conference, refers to "a French news service," interrupts
any in-place correspondent's story with a question which'd keep. This is not accident, but
        patent
envy of reporters, generals who, exhibiting understanding, can say a thing
succinctly, get facts right, be clear (even) about implications. So these filters, concerned
        faces
between us and the news are cultural, interfaces between event or comment
and the man in the diner, imagined as needing hitch and stumble phrases
(now let's get this straight, Peter), everyone jockeying for importance while
considerably behind their perspectives and in a sense unnoticed a war goes on,
continues as they say to their Showdown logo. Mr. Saddam "lobs" missiles
at Israel, his guard Praetorian, our planes armada, as if Patton's mind scleroticized
chugs on, the Somme an odor, lingering, not even horrified that to his auditors
any intrusion is a pincer movement, footage of babies wrapped in gas masks what war
is all about, put in, that's to say, that perspective
while from us it's an unholy joy to deny a name and employer to what by this slip
becomes our man in Baghdad, whose bombardment footage we play and play.
Take time out for breath here, Peter, Dan. Mike Wallace has to sound acute,
Cronkite wise, football, election-night the metaphors we run on.
Peace plans will be unveiled. Everyone says gonna. That night the man "breaking" the story
he heard on Israeli radio had them all, patently, wanting it to be London and Edward
R. Murrow, even my cat miaowing like a voiceover to Senator Simpson,
whose striped tie and opinions I admire. Is it anxiety to be in the know
or unemployment fear that makes the anchorperson seem more endangered,
so far from any universe of fact or thought, than people ducking shrapnel.
Wear your beeper. News can happen anywhere, "What has transpired over there, uh,
        thus far."

My Spring Break: five poems

Knickknackery

The man (is) the woman (is) I kept seeing at the starts
of poems, statements blatant, flat, as a cow in a field (is),
brown suede above, cream below, tippable decanter of cowhood
that put on the board will be obediently self for you so not its self
but yourselfed, delft, the poem a souvenir, memory napkin, of
say the time you with grandmum went with cousins, nephews to the
small town outside San Antonio where they sit legs wide apart
like Brancusi andirons. There, an allusion not infinitely arcane (is)
on the board to balance out the rustics, with a grace of their own
perhaps ungenerously kept. Remington observed in all this brightness

for himself how odd the shadows under horses, themselves colors (are)
all infinitely backlit, a study for all your life how, active,
nearly in flight, animals take light. We pass a welder
in a truck. This is Texas. Look on the cows
as dance partners, datable, or prophets in some vulgar mural
in a tin shed advertised at roadside, Life of Christ bigger
even than in your bible. Take these things as like the cows,
deliberate stylizations of human need, here to feed
you on russet or the color a collar of foam on a Guinness
makes on a Guinness. Crowcroft says there's a nematode that lives
between the layers or cork of a German beermat, nowhere else
and you may think of cows as (put) on land to be observed
or written about like drab doomed souls in poems by reference only
forced to begin, as County Line has mechanical musicians which
play when you activate their 78s, a logo on their stands, Chan's
wax museum in which any standing figure hides self and weapon
till lights go out, the slither of cloth then, giggle of highschool
students creeping toward the cow. We're all victims of other people's intent
even if their designs on us are innocent. What I want to do
when I see those cows so innocent of wishing (to be) in another field
I wish to grab them by a curled stiff tail turned porcelain, my other
hand gone giant just where the faces change color and tip them
till milk pours over the field as if it were a bowl of oatmeal
from a throat white and smooth as if dunked in bisque glaze and fired.

Saints' Roost Bible Shoot

When you've seen the antique church, the
courthouse and the Owens boot
emporium all that Clarendon
has left to show's the Bible Shoot
held every other Fourth unless
it's on a Sunday. We defer
it then to an adjacent year
as what the local saints prefer.
We trust their judgment with a little
j more than the other one
which likewise we would like put off
until the Fourth and Shoot are done.
Tradition's such an awkward thing
if Saturday's the time that you've
got free from cattleherding for
the doings widows most reprove.
Our Stetsons brushed, the long white coats
we wear to keep the dust at bay
banged white and chaps too full of blood
and sweat put up, our Saturday
is sacred too, and so we prop
some Bibles up between two nails
on posts. We're given one shot each

with a forty-five, like heads or tails.
Few hit the book. If you do the score
is tallied with a knife of horn
to excavate the bullet where
the page that stopped it's yet untorn.
Of course if you come out the other
side you get a ninety-three
but this with a black powder load
we all consider gaucherie.
The trick is to look at the text
the lead could find no passage through,
the local superstition is
it read aloud applies to you.
Our sport has this much point. Say Whitley
drills halfway through Psalms. We buy a
drink for him and razz the man
whose vigor stops at Jeremiah.
A motel Bible works just fine
but it seems to us the penetration's
better through limp leather, gilt
edged and damn the illustrations.
The saints decry our Bible Shoot
the preacher swears, the widow's vexed
but each of us lives by his own
impenetrable Bible text.

Syllabary for Doris Cross

who needs none, *Expire Expressly* currently above her mantel, "done/retroacting/to ask/
   lā la/
the meaning/so that nothing is left to be/inferred" white letters on black complete
as it stands. You hand me a sheet, words with page refs and your own definitions for once,
swinging pretty free, the talk of sculpture—Stella's *Moby-Dick* cast aluminum, magnesium
painted pieces—and Malevich, wanting to see theory or autobiography by him, and Mallarmé
so we look, Valéry's *Masters & Friends* and today in another shop *Teste* like new in
   Princeton paper.
Santa Fe stocks Baudelaire and Verlaine (but has a good art store). It's that when
(I told you) the typewriter makes the lines break, wrap around they won't even in twelve-point
set type, so that's a choice you'll start making or leave to the printer (who should be told
everything). Leave nothing to chance, you who saw any dictionary column as a column, so
close to verse, the "definition" something like a line underslung to fit *its* needs.
John Hollander proposed a notation for increasingly violent line-ends, a calculus
from take off to ham-burger, lovely effect Marianne Moore gets with a hyphen to
keep her syllable count. If you worked in clay it'd be what cracks you leave, allow for
   shrinkage
as when my Papillon statuette's chest tuft cracked just a bit, glazed, improving the effect
   of fur.
My long lines exceed a page width deliberately. What won't fit drops down, indents.
Clio wearing the lavender stole of your daughter's weave in the audiologist's
is, you say, an angel—I add to it your "Art is continuous." You like what I blank out, the

print from my poem showing through as vertical lines. Heighten the darks, you say. I do
    with India ink
and in your back room make lavender of permanent rose and Antwerp blue for stole's
two verticals, white with a bit of pale lemon, almost a strontium, on the hair,
mixed with rose for a touch of color on face and hands, varnish pulling the print through
the paper without smearing ink, then gel to glue the folded sheet to itself, my name
a floating vertical by the waiting room's chair's Craft Period squared-off arm
(tinted with a bit of raw umber from a tube that sprang a leak), then gel and varnish
on a canvas, sketch pressed on, gelled down. No wonder here, just a record of a conversation.
You ask is sculpture an artifact? I say probably not. You say what is it then and I say
    probably a vice.
We like it all pretty now, like Scarpa's architecture plans, the land itself in faded ink,
structure in pencil and wash, covered-passage mound Tiepoloan, post-Palladio with scat
details rendered anywhere they fit. I'd say the problem is fluidity of grid, words
Paul of St. Victor'd stud a page with and buckle in with other words, vs. carving
cutting as you go, the fixity in either case under what you see, a rootedness of root.
You tire of that and want Versailles made of cardboard, round painted pillars,
Quaker Oats boxes in a row, in the last one's planter's hat a downy feather, panache.

Yellowbird in Ildefonso

paintbrush in hand, red-tipped, applied
thin liquid glaze to the off-ivory buff
pot he was working on and showed us how
you rub it with an agate (his with a long extension,
tape-wrapped) to get the shiny finish
on his flaring conical-based necked vase
with a lid, two blobby bears walking
not at all like krater handles on the edge
or rim where the neck begins curving in
these bears, one per side, one walking toward
you, one away. A flat lid has on it
triumphantly, as on a monument, a third.
He had (he showed us) a round pot he
built full around, a closed globe his thumb
pressed in the top of, explaining to us the bear
is healer, tutelary deity, as he meditated toward Black Mesa
saw the pot as that—butte from the road
spectrally dark against brush-dotted lighter
sharper hills, saw or felt the pot, in his hands,
as the mesa. Another hollowed pot fell on its side;
picking it up he saw it as a bear. The limbs
press to a ridge transverse to spine he first
noticed in his dog, bang-on for bear anatomy
and now he's this pot, scooping in in an
Ildefonsan way to simplest neck, the clay just curving
at the edge of air, this with a lid on, plop
with bear, too grand to be a handle or a finial
yet friendly (and the top not heavy at all,
hollow, he said) so you've this black pot

or covered vase, polished with sandpaper and agate
the bear, in a sense one bear, making a circuit
finished at the top, the mouth slightly open, all
their eyes just dimpled in, black from being packed
with dried cow chips to pull out oxygen
from the red glaze in exchange for carbon
to blacken bears, and lid, and bear.

The Beauty of All Reasons

This is not a poem, or perhaps to be a poem. It is "about" a big collage, maybe
three feet by 2½, horizontal, we just made—two days to do it—in Doris's back
workroom, a good white poster board attached to the (clothcovered) wall with push pins.
There was, in the middle of this white page, a large photograph pushpinned on, the edges
      curling
in a way Doris liked and I didn't. I saw a box insert, offwhite cardboard with round holes
      in rows
as if to keep tempera jars upright, and thought (since we spoke of Rauschenberg) it would be
      attractive up,
and then saw a browning note in Doris's writing, just names of colors. Arranging the two
on a white ground was almost a silly "problem," but no problem's silly attacked.
I said we could glue the cardboard where two edges folded over just a bit, verticals.
"Why don't you?" My rubber glue was at the motel so she found a big tube we snipped the
      nozzle of,
and I pushed from its flared neck toward a hammer handle held against my chest—
lacking the aluminum gun for it—while Doris held and moved the board. Looked good.
She found an even browner strip with writing on, the octopus as Homer's polyp, her first
      "chart,"
and Yes-glued that under the cardboard and color list—Doris loves vertical rectangles—
      and
so I said Doris, what we need is an envelope from a gallery, addressed to you with their
      return address
printed. She found an envelope from Germany with a typewriter-generated beetle enclosed
      we pulled
nearly halfway out and glued all down. What else? a square snippet from a working drawing,
just words, saying continue this figure (arrow) on a white ground. So then I drew a teapot
around where we then glued a teabag she found—we didn't like that so the vandalized
working sketch (of a tall vertical, one of her two-column revisions of dictionary pages)
went there, and on the righthand side a tall tall figure in black on more brownish-yellowed
      paper,
flush right we'd say in printing, and she said What do you think about drapery? and found
a length of cheesecloth I glued and pushpinned on, all folds (over the teapot spout). Her typed
poem from bottom left got moved, the scotch tape so old we Yessed it, just below
the envelope; I slammed in a freeform shape in Winsor Red just before the curtain's
      white-on-white formality, a
dribble of it running down a thread tacked down from the drape top with a stroke of glue
      brush
and added sideways at the bottom a pencil rendering of a bean can, most elegant.
Later she said (I probably wouldn't like this) what if we glued the curtain flat, I did, and
      added STUDIO #1 in not

so interesting pencil at the top. A green push pin in the curtain replaced with a green
   painted dot.
Doris finds a thin wood triangle, can we use this? I glue it to make a bottom righthand corner
to the paper and cardboard initial (squarish) composition, the wood coated with Yes,
stuck on too far, moved left, triangular image left in glue I at once outline in soft pencil
in honor of collages with drawn and glued on squares and parts of squares. We prop it
with a mop handle, at once deciding that diagonal into the room needn't stay
through to exhibition.
The dried curtain neither this nor that, she says it needs a diagonal, here . . . I say that pencil
won't even take (it didn't), though she pulled a flattened fold or two up, impatient slash.
   I have
(mad gleam) silver paint. Aluminum. We'd thought to do a second panel flat black from
   Rustoleum.
So I did a bit of silver edging at the bottom, touch at the side, then we tried black and
   combinations,
nothing really interesting, and Doris proposes as something novel ripping the curtain off.
   I do
a mock one in Rustoleum black—over even the green dot—and it looks good, as we say,
   "It's good."
I say, how about a little pale blue *here,* bottom righthand corner of the (now merely
   calligraphic)
curtain, try it, maybe more, she says, I add two strokes of the big round brush, charged with
   white and a touch of cerulean blue
mixed in a disposable muffin tin, one pocket already mineral spirits and aluminum
   Rustoleum,
which spills as I add blues. More, she says, confessing it's a vice—under the envelope,
a bit on the far left (up a bit more, and down), and slopping in these powdery blues I
having added BOX FETISH in charcoal above the polyp horizontal obliterate
STUDIO #1 and all is better, much improved. I've typed Doris's and my names at right
angles to each other, the way we signed it the first day now covered over with bean can,
   one fits
perfectly at the base of my drawn right triangle that butts against the real one, so
it's signed, better in a way for being typed.

Love Poem

I want your hair weave when you cut it out. For days setup lines for
the Yugoslav Phrase Book, now this (Blazier to Sara), near in
effect to Brautigan's "You bring the bleach," if that's his, no
reason to remember that author particularly; not my period. I mean,
a taste for Brautigan, all those identical book covers, hoping to
be Hershey's, flawed motive for those of us who, growing up in
Detroit a few years after hippies proper, those who became hippies,
looked to us like *having* to have one particular finned fender, simply
not, in us, a need. Answered to none. If cars came with huge screw lids
you could, rotating, climb out of, our mouths Vs, that'd incorporate
Wells's notion . . . something like wet liver coming out of ("emerging,"
significant verb) from cream and off pink enamel with chrome trim, this
would be a use and eventually a need, as the remake *Blob* incorporates
half-eaten people and artifacts, or brooder victim *Alien* losers in

frangible plastic-sugar matrices. It's been suggested matrimony's
etymology get looked up. The passivity of *being* invaded is like this,
and so, young women wrap thread (pulling it through itself like a
single knot) to make series of colors binding like cheap beads a few
strands of hair, and stiffening them too, this product of boredom in
a classroom where, rooms away, younger women with their own hair weaves
study Indians, prepare a Sioux newsletter, draw wigwams and think of
wearing deer, pony, eating dog, everything you own that's flexible made
like chainmail or fishscale weave. It's the warm, thoughtless days
behind these, sound of pots you've just made trapping cooler air,
drying in sun, that make anything you do a little like a slightly
crosseyed concern, say indigestion or mildest headache (almost somebody
else's, being *around* someone who has a headache or is a pot) that leads
to remarks so offhand they are Slavic. You say such things to the air,
of which who hears them is an interruption, such intimacy as people
fishing off the same pier might be said to have, if it were expectably
unnecessary to say to each other anything like it, the being brutally there
with you enough to draw the remark you'd say almost as soon to a tile wall.
Say that any thou, ascribing otherness to auditor, concedes too much, our
will more bent on sighing than discourse, on pouring, for the moment, soap
granules into the rounded-corner opening than any concentration you'd think
would linger on blue towels curled tight like rope, square ends of teeshirt
or napkin, these no more in the mind than funny sayings on them if though
absent entertainable convention. You don't want the hair weave, that segment
of dark umber braided (knowing that to cut it makes a stickup bit), but in
a way covet the caring built into its dit-dah-dit segmentable wove length,
perhaps as you want life to continue or something general as the recognizable,
some quality never to be abstracted from a moment cherishable because ununique.

The Limits of Art

Eskimo masks in Menil with green hair
or African animal heads so large
they become masks for the body
mask intent, the necessary eyeholes
down around the nose, say,
tucked in where Picasso put
nose lines in to define cheeks.
Busking's the word to have as analogue
masking, vigorous activity as when the Hopi
come out of the ground, scaring youths
with hair, *hair,* through holes in wood
or as in the Santa Fe kachina buffalo
glued on. This patter masks the metal heads
in Guatemala, there to offset lovely pale
peach-blue eyed additions, mask like a
false nose, the nordic mimicked then back
in Africa to serial decorations, brass nailheads
like tattooing, trafficlight medicine man's high visage,
Tardis extension no longer like the skull at all.

It's as if the Eskimo animals dance crawling,
Gorer's Africans rather punching air, but
what's different outside Moose, Elk, Shriner's
the peering at we do, immune to trickster's pinch,
spectacle of these things clad in hexagonal clothing,
tabards, milling around you to the didgery-doo, big clay
faces shapeless, First Men, as if lye victims or proto-
albinids watching us by rushlight, the tassels and bead strips
like ours, those heads like flintlocks aimed at us
swaying like a bear, snouted, loaded.
You go from this to something post-*Lycidas,* Comus a
masquerade in which all witty pleasure's Caliban
you know from their not touching him's contaminant,
cherub in the wall, Batchelder's moulded halloweeen ape
let right into their Boston corridor plaster, so
a trip to the bathroom's observed, black getup
surely he "donned" to go with his found-material mask,
plastic's punched holes like some transmission drink-holder
or Mozartian basket for the head, no place for eyes
but a pendant airbubble packing strip coming out
like a mouth or Punch puppeteer's translucent screen
and up top, a deepsea creature's artifice, the bent arm of
a battery reading light for staying up on trains
or in beds, not meant for a star stuck on
the head like a flagpole in a groin socket
for some Fourth celebration, Civil-War antique
and a rod of office, complicated by a plate or ribbons,
so chilly Mr. Freeze in black walks up to you
the day artists expect costume, but this is real.

Surrealism at Menil

is a dozen Cornell boxes including homages à ballet and the renaissance pinball, broken
panes; all frames ached to have been found, exhibiting themselves like faces in Dante's
hell's lambent light, blue or pale peach-rose liquids in apothecary bottles never green or
      bright yellow,
specimens always white, tinted by pickle. In an adjacent chamber nail fetishes, very good
      ones,
stood (vertically if little men) furred with nails bigheaded and bent, a few blades, rusted to one
tone like Gillettes in a built-in motel tile slot. We frame it all as art, Magritte's "Pipe" and
      the big Ernst
King Crab chessplayer faux primitif but antlered in strong front light, giving you the choice
of ignoring the shadows on his thin chest. White rooms with tile, set of white tiled
things, industrielle, a nice de Kooning Attic study and a big one in the hall wet smears of
      madder making
at their thinnest pink, in general opaque vs. transparent paint a kind of theme
as in a way Magritte's bronze trunk and ax, folding coffin in chaise longue prepared you
like a baptistry or confession boxes for Cornell lorgnette studies so much the scale
and materials of one's glasses through which we peer at boxed frame windows
in mouse blue velour through which a book or book-shape wrapped in dark-blue velvet, tied

in powder-blue twine knotted to rectangles takes up the box space under tiny mirrored twin.
Oh yes, if we'd seen a fire extinguisher on any wall it would have been art, the urinal
nearly, hard to find on Sul Ross as the building itself, vertical pale boards like a Christo
mock-illusive matchboard look-in floor, charming as de Chirico tea biscuits in front of stuff.

Lunch at the Bon Ton

was not my paying and that colored it, a refrigerated distance (my pen
lent out), already losing the pale bluegray Conan's booth, Sara to my (my)
right not smoking, careful not to smoke because Chris said she looks
like *Beetlejuice's* Lydia when she does, the new *Chronicle* (cover ink an Indian yellow,
best of all colors that really used to be made from crystals of Yak urine, the
obligatory "News of the Weird" pause, hideous Groening, all standard folk appeals, on our
plates circular as Euclid rectangular pizza, the ridge of crust geology, the talk idle,
who wrote what on the wall. At nine the magazine man, to his right a *US News* poster on
Best Colleges, prepped students how to sell, McIntosh and Castleberry, tall, holding the
     oilcloth
dummy order up for us to read, that rolls on rods like a report to Caesar,
the promise of ice cream instead of lunch, of class, no more for us these regions free of
personalized endeavor, as when in Tourtelotte I showed my special ed kids how to make
houses with peaked ends a folded roof fit on, on it, notched square, a chimney.
Doors bent. Silos were cylinders with flat cone hats.
I cut my pizza (ridge end) like a fringe in serried notches then in an inch and three quarters,
to separate like toast fingers with a crunchy end, all this my comfort for a morning
unsettled having attacked dignity from a direction unexpected, Carl fed token ice cream,
     topped, to make it real to all.
Today was about food not for itself, Jan's apple eaten while he did geometry,
the hollow sound of apple bitten in against palate not there for him or a discounted datum.
Tom came in with lunch and found the room too quiet. Sara's back, walking quite elegantly
in thready cutoffs, barefoot, ear to nose relation (through a fringe of hair, I notice) like a lion.
Someone broke Chris's typewriter (over lunch). All these absences, usually from class,
occurred at lunch, and people who went to see the World War II plane couldn't find it,
tie tucked in my shirt pocket to keep sauce off it, plate wiped clean.

Celluloid

that we saw
including Selznick's
rolls in Charles
Bell's film collection
to be stored
in a bunker, the
stories go, flames
in barrels, Laurel &
Hardy up, space-saving
motion since the stuff
does weigh, is

transparent, related
to *Cellulose*
that was the title
when this was
commissioned. The
wipable collar and
cuffs pulled this
from thinking on
not being able to
digest something
to film as a

repository of
images, like bullets
shaped like soldiers.
I call and hear
Lee's 95 lbs.
and still gets lots
of *Temblor* mail.
Fortunately his best
reading's on videotape.
My teacup with
a tiny roach
(not usual) in
says Vicious Power
Hungry BITCH
exclamation mark.
The animal suiciding
headforward on typewriter
keys gets caps at last
by accident. Lives built
on spiral molecules
can't eat (without bacteria
in the stomach) cellulose,
some termite clear

as blown glass, the
photograph retained.
Clio's Galveston
great-aunt gave us
twenties shots including
three lovely children
"lost in the storm,"
immedicable loss
usual but their
presences, so much
not for history, not
needing margin to be
power hungry in
attacked by acid
in the mounting board
black-paper faced
gray, brown probably
once ivory, not ever
quite the right size
their clothes then
but you know their
bodies were like ours.

Analogies of Influence

I'm facing a painting, not feeling much of the confrontational feeling that's usual fronting art,
small canvas, vertical, a long beltlike object (strap with a loop, or buckle) angling up over
   blueblack blob
and to its left a large very recognizable fork, scrofulous green with wax blobs on it, and iron
filings, I'm told, bits of sparkle, ah red where underorange shows through, massive navel
   on the
belt a rivet, it's deformed scissors, rabbit under just a black and Prussian blue outline
   filled in
with professional offhand smear of green, pasteled with yellow just visible under, touch
   of red
as if an eye or two, just left of the smudge perhaps meant for an eye, on the other side of the
   scissors'
loop for the fingers a cactus really foot and shin of humanoid tall as the canvas, blueblack
   hair,
face smeared as Nolde, squiggle like intestines down the jumper front, das yellow key
   design (chunk
chunk chunk chunk) down both the scissor shanks, this pale gray cloud top left, above
   everything, "stretching"
if you like, really extending not dramatic at all into, "between" blades like legs on a falling
   Icarus,
that's it, white ground, the left less whitey-blue, brown pits in canvas showing through.
What's to say, arms on a figure yellow green as canned asparagus, colors in general dark or
   light, forma formant.

An ant didn't do it but Chris Blazier who signed CB lower right so low its frame can have
    no lap, the fork
reminding me of a local restaurant's large upright one for a sign, variously impaling lips,
    a fish,
modulable. They ran a contest with xeroxed upright fork, tines ending short for what to put
    on it and (this
being Austin) what won's a globe, wide slot like grin through South America, on the high side
stuck *on* it EAT in neon. This is Austin. Globes always win. The fork is almost the only
nonweapon implement. Austin thinks any icon is an Uzi. There is a red piano stuck canted
above a shop, all its edges (lovely curves) outlined at night in red neon. The trick for a
    symbol you can eat is call it an emblem, the bell
on our cat's collar a "sign" we may stalk. The fork is not an enlargement of a restaurant
    utensil, old-fashioned milkbottle shops selling milk.
The fork's freestanding, like a gun not being used, or Millet farmer (resting) saying the
    Angelus, not pictured resting.
The fork in a painting may refer to still-life habit of assembled goods, but as floated on canvas
floats free of its own size *and* iconicity, becomes tasteless fork, with wax on, not to eat.

Advice to Poets

Do you sob in short lines? The
manic-depressive leader of the
poetry group said I see, you're
one of those who stays on the sidelines
reporting, her point being I'm
involved in noninvolvement, the low-
risk end of writing while she
always ready to spin away
becoming god, surprised
she's not recognized (let out
she'd scan the papers for her name)
told me this: she'd run once
through the radio dial and she'd be
caught up on everything. And knows
no counting, says how can you *do*
that to yourself, constrict the
imagination that makes her
like god, celebrity. She draws
as well, it saved her life, was
her salvation. I'd
use the word salvific
if she'd let me. Oh put
it all in a batter bowl,
knead and spin, make a
pizza of her life, of mine
abstract her words, and
fierce. She says they put
you in when you want to be part
of the cosmos, a little room
like a foot-long hot dog

on a tortilla. It makes you
too angry to write. She thinks
Blake, those English eccentrics have
problems like hers.

Post-Keynesian Repp Poem

Kleinzahler's remark in *Brief 9* tears it for me, Waldenbooks and
Iowa Workshops "symptoms of . . . profit's disconnectedness from real production," in
exactly the tone people'd think paper money less real than gold, miss silver in quarters.
It's simply not how things go, "real production" (chickens, things you wipe windshields
    with)
not rewarded as formerly, as if Carlyle on the Consumer Nexus. What'd'you want, the
grocer to feed the pigs he smokes? We were just visiting friends with Plymouth Rock gray
chickens walking over their deck, pecking the fey boat "like popcorn" Zero made their kids
(it flips in storms), so, they look after him too. You get us closer to those
entrepreneurs on Guadalupe, framed velvet with earrings, items made from nickels
that when *I* was a kid you went to the Village for, to the shop smelling of leather
full of *real* vests, hats, belts—holsters, too, with snaps, for my circus derringers—
where if you put your foot on a hide they'd cut around it with a linoleum knife
hooked like Death of a Thousand Cuts, and add fine laces like SPQR up a woman's foot,
    all kinda
custom off the street, they'd stain your belt edge and talk to you almost like a relation.
All right, you're bored. Though to write so of parties after readings suggests
you're plugged in still, yourself. Your verbs exhibit decay; all you make
fun of sticks to you. Highschool civics is good for what you think
poets you meet should be. I used to say most magicians are like tie salesmen,
in the back of my mind the wonderful scissors you'd get at Abbott's (the
old Detroit shop) that *sounded* good though welded shut you'd go at
a guy's tie with, hijinks of the conventions I never went to. Your tie, sir, with
its horizontal stripes suggests it's already cut. You worry in such company about
being mistaken for a timeserver on panels, or Jerome with his books on what
it feels like to create. Why expressing this employ their verbs? If it were me
I'd advance on the sandalmaker's open collar, lift his imaginary tie and snip.

Black Cat in Garden

Black, mostly Persian, built like a shovel of cement
slopped on masonite, the hair adhesive as a sloth's
(perhaps porous) hence Cobweb for a name, moves almost as if
about to squat, the progress serried flattenings, prudence and
jingo, gunboat. We met a man whose granpa sold
horses out of Texas to the English for the Boers, that set of deals
so goodnatured, outdoor advertising, less historically come on
than hardware (he jumps for flies, ignores a lizard), the
woodpile's small twisted branches stairs, installation, environ.
We want to kill something, are on a long red braided leash

behind the mulch block cinder block, in undappled shadow, the red retriever barks
us to a tree the gold eyes look at me around.
Smell more plants, explore the middle, every bit of leaf litter
on Bagheera's undercarriage while the
child next door climbs the ladder in the tree, its father
tennis shoes and jeans empties trash into the garbage can
just outside the white fence like the ones you keep a horse behind.
There are no flowers visible though tiny ones must occur
but a cat of this dimension in a garden makes it feel floral.
Beneath my feet, tail on my feet by the asbestos shingle wall
we are a musketeer waiting for the killer butterfly we've heard will go
a distance from you in a straight line, to turn and charge, unbattable,
to be attacked by something small unlikely by asbestos wall.

Instances of Martha Graham

To me the most interesting instances of Martha Graham are her appearances, like
    Jove-stones,
in *Dance to the Piper* at crucial moments in de Mille's life, there with
a gnomic utterance strained from years of private suffering and rehearsal of pieces
implicating a woman's body in unexpected relations, sinking down like a compass on its
    point,
one straight leg in torsion, a remark made to music, kind of Aeschylus made of
homage to Dickinson, some elm in O'Neill's *Desire,* a Voltaire of dancers, head by
    Roubilliac.
There's a feature in the Litchfield *Times* using her to beat Madonna with by a columnist
who should've known better than to mix professionals. It's like using Nietzsche to beat
    Whitman,
possible but not desirable. MG lived long enough to take an hon. degree from Harvard
for giving dance an inward nature, as O'Neill tried with our drama, process oddly in tune
with Gershwin Bandbox musicals, Ed Wynn on Ziegfeld's stage, and light picked out your
    color,
and you worked. I've Guérard on art for its own sake to read
along with bombthrowers, Hill on Cromwell's men, Sorel, lacking Huneker on Stirner, but
there's that quality of light (slop) on a stage then, quite a big one justified by seats and
    boxes, the kind
that'd empty into Delmonico's, nothing of it left now except Asti's where the waiters still
    sing,
the danger of anything breaking into dance or song, the little man eating his boutonniere,
    cigar.
You've a vulgar lower end, dancers' feet bleeding, as we know, menstruation kicking in
    onstage,
and no one caring at the level of composition that the act of it is occurring, in some diner.
Tonight I've trouble remembering names of acts I've nearly memorized, odd that dancers
(turns perhaps) aren't acts as such outside Imogene Coca's Swan Lake, the point still
that even astringent artists like Wallace Stevens have moments flipping the paper out to
    hold it open
by changing the creases of its ephemeral pages.

Dog in Chair

not quite three pounds extends the forelegs delicate as Florentine slippers
in old woodcuts, eyes shut in the small brown head, neat snout, for once
the giant pointed ears laid back and losing the Vampyr outline
in fringes, like a hairstyle just no longer popular, the ringlets
women wore with white cotton shirts, frilled dresses, loose
vermicelli spirals. We've had both dog and cat to school,
Phoebe for first-day kindergarteners, passed from hand to hand,
her attention evenly distributed. Now she moves against me
like a restless glove, the cat visible a room away, its pointed
ears like Batman's. The dog is white. The black cat's upside-down,
all alone, paws up, shaved belly nearly dark. Its little bell
foretells motion. The Papillon's at rest. We listen for the cat.
What is it like to be so near a pet, "close to it," you forget
it's there without forgetting it? Like a decoration on your sock.
She's flipped to the other side, paws folded as if midrun. Yet she
seldom imagines chasing in her sleep. We have a photograph of her
held up in a hand nearly as large as herself. The scale of her,
not much larger than a travel iron, makes her miniature, a "toy"
smaller than the fluffies Fragonard painted women playing with
in boudoirs, old hands at sealed-letter intrigues. They say when
Marie Antoinette was topped a dog or two of this breed crept
from under her skirts. They're brave enough for it to've been so,
carried in panniers all the way from Spain, the route Cézanne took
whose cardplayers and bathers did without a dog this size,
size of the plaster Cupid he did at least once, thrust up through,
the torso turning, a picture plane as if some laundress toweling for Degas.
Our dog when wet is smaller than a squirrel, shivers in its Harvard towel,
kindly with its Yoda ears but puzzled that it's wet. She is
ideal dry, the moisture thrown like darts from a porcupine,
lap stain big as a loincloth from her drying.

Who Sometime Did Me Seek

Leafing through Kilmer's *Catholic Poets,* titles like "At Palomar," Jesuits named Walsh
good enough to print, then Dowson, skrittering recollection of the Modernists' *Catholic
       Anthology,* why should we
care what those old Norfolk pieties, American "religious" thought on any subject,
gongorist tormentings of the infant Christ as Master of the World, cheap paradox
in sentence sounds and diction quite as cheap. "And yet I often do," Larkin said
of churches, Edwards showing us slides of one in a town he didn't try to pronounce,
lovely as baked Alaska, inside Gautama Pancrator, earlobes and triple crown
cradles Christ Declined, bent from his cross, or a robed Virgin's long face
so unexpected it's like Warhol or Dodgson's sheep-shopkeeper, gaah, these poems
on hosts on exhibition, martyrs named, Balliol ballads by Belloc, angels of the house . . .
It's true, like Catholic philosophy it has to come from the philosopher in you, wrong to
address the walking on water and drama of Christian drama. (If you
write poems you don't say Well, somebody will like them, waffle about use.)
The Ildefonsan craftsman made a vase with bears perambulating on the bellied shelf of it,

and one on top, flat cover like a pyx, black from firing in a reducing atmosphere,
purgatorial if you like, of dried cow-feces. The church they show is new and dull, the old one
judging from photographs charming, like a hill built up around Stonehenge, their map
colored with felt pens to something beyond utility. Rousseau's dreaming Ethiop
calls up like Magritte's objects in clay under the sleeper this pin-eyed lion,
source of power in Stevens's glass of water, Energy directed by Appetite.
You write of religion in it not about it, all relics first class from something etheric run through,
fluid mana taught you by sisters of St. Joseph, IHM, ordinary as the day.
Memoria looking in marble mirror no more polished than a bar top
"sees" nothing at all, adopts the attitude of Contemplating a Reflection, not something
          perused
as one looks in one's heart, transcribing it. Murdoch writes a novel about The Bell,
magic medieval, Golding does The Spire, Lowell addresses the Mother
in the window when he does, provoking Plath's Papa and here's Winwar's book,
Pre-Raphaelite gossip, written before she did Dannunzio. I'll maybe never see
Rheims from the air, Cologne, Florence. I painted old Concepcion
twice in one day (badly), Bellocian activity to *have* done, the badness not my intent
they with a Maltese Christ, elevated, wonderful. You can come to a church to make art
and it not happen. It doesn't feel like one's pursued yet in church shade . . .
you've spent so much of your time growing up rattling Latin to ae priest's
it's like poor Burns raised to the Holy Fair, all yawping townsmen
making love to Calvinzac. The corruption there, if it was, was one's attention
kicking in and out, toying with value, was entertainment, pillows you'd not
see at home, marimba played with rubber ball on stick for the Elevation.
(The protestants had endless hymnals stuck in slats in pews.) Memory had
no part beyond the rote retention, though meant, of the server's answers.
You can use a calculator without being able to make one. It was lambs
bland in marble or wood painted to look like it with crosshilt sword right through,
visible in its results as Oskar's tin-drum assault on Danzic
a shower of—what? the result, dandelion Christ coming down to drink, the infant Blake,
not that I gave a nickel for his psyche, carried shoulder-high by discredited Christopher
and boys wear this tube of cloth, ending in lace, somehow almost Greek.

The Perfect World [first approximation]

One goes to a yard sale not to buy things but to see tired objects in a stressed relation. Hope
makes you want to see things lost like condensation on the fiesta pitcher full of Koolaid;
words stay ordinary as cameras without their cheap plastic cases, the cheapening
effect of naming objects. Nothing is a list. The patient on the operating table, as Eliot
          observes,
is an arrangement, and objects are our kindly feelings toward them. So "objects"
is itself a joke, delicious pretense of objectivity in some cool Beuys room dedicated
by the word (or hung chalkboards standing for theory) to exhibition. The point
is that any theory will do. The pig is the granular surface of the football, also the word is.
A show in D-Art in Dallas included Greg Metz's pig's head in a coffin, and as O'Hara's
          loved
days go by went by it smelt like a funeral parlor with failed air conditioning,
the structure of the pig so useful for dissection also like it at the level of bacterium effluvium.
                              Rauschenberg's painting
of a Civil War coffin would not be improved particularly with a touch of this smell,

but you can see how the carcase might wish to define itself, Chamberlain mortuary of
    wonderful car colors
underwritten by chrome. There's a way of being at home with things. One
very nice blond gent sat barefoot in shorts in shadow from a square canopy
he'd raised on poles, the blue plastic with waffle grid like no blue in nature now a tarp
playing a harmonica. I grabbed an easel and painted him in front of his boring house, using
any color for shadow on his siding, no *matter* what anything was, all for sale
and yesterday put that canvas in the yard sale the whitehaired German woman runs
on weekends (with books on Heidegger in her bins) so there you've program music, an
Illustrated Man if his tattoos were ecorché, kidneys and ribs crawling around anywhere
    they'd fit. Similarly a blender,
holy thing, any "appliance" woven cord (our mockups when I was a child were string
incorporating neither process nor tail but the move from plaid effect of clothcovered wire
    to ravelable twine)
are how they felt as interruptions of kitchen space dull as a football field.
The word's not elements if your collage is the world and what if you collage
the *notion* collage, greet any ordering as represented neither by itself nor map thereof,
like the book I bought for fifty cents in pale tomato covers, Heidegger's Ground of Ground
no more important than the quarters in the wallet, not "mine" because transposed from
    sunlit bin
to car to house, "shelved" in my head's museum without shelves. Some things
you face demand no retrieval, aren't objects of surmise. The toaster with electric flameshaped
bulbs stuck up its slots says on its plate VESUVIUS, the name you'd see
in Washington Square espresso shops in metal bolted on, just a remark no different
from Salvator Rosa eagle nesting on the polished hemisphere, apparent symbol really just
the metal eagle like a Mickey Mouse camera or clock, happening to be that, no statement
    intended
about Mickey's Time, the way it is my Heidegger. So ownership is going to the yard sale
    at all;
what we see there, all of it, is ours.
                        Say otherwise it doesn't matter, the pipe in a Picasso, so soon after
Magritte's Ce n'est pas un pipe, Jack Horner school of plum, Spoerri's lunch tables
glued and wired in place (forks, breadcrusts, wine stains) elevated to museum wall,
    post-prandial icon,
interested a little in saying this is this. Here we've things, found or made no matter
which say what they say anyway, you loved me when I was a lion, now I'm next a lamb
like separating, most accidentally, the movie poster from the film going on inside. You
    could redo
Wilbur's old title, Love Calls Us to the Things of This World to things call us, remind us
how much we love them anyway, the mystery Robert Frost remarks, suspecting it,
how much it is they haven't to deserve. The lovely pin that snaps overall suspender
to its bib grows on us, we peer, lean, have a good time, these are all things we know.

The Dryness of Realism

was meant to be a ten-pager for my Seventh Grade, in exchange for theirs
and I'd this in mind on the informative information, things as one of my
students put it you really don't want to know that Balzac (and Bennett,
Mansfield) will put out. Edward Batchelder at Houghton, Mifflin confessed
an urge to people his desk with dimestore frames, the token relatives there to show them off

still in them, generic daughter, dog, wife photogenic in wine-red sweater,
wearing her age well. So realism could eventually discount itself, say merely chambermaid,
Cafe Royal, points made like a Duchamp bicycle (as Marjorie Perloff says
ramming its vertical through a stool), this need to name beyond particularity—Greta,
the servant's name was Greta—and oh we feel the bored polish on bannister rail, how
little decisions, the tin being low, get made belowstairs while we, relieved of wraps
proceed expanding, the moisture of bundled transit a new interval, like wine in restaurant
     glass, a too officious
waiter approaching, up Yeats's Eliot's stairway to Joyce's concert rooms, the young UTD
man in borrowed fig there on sufferance, mingling with protestants, an oddshaped room in
     far-off London with
on its wall a strongjawed dryadess, all eyes, the furniture all butted, crafts stuff you sprawl
     in, Pine Factory
or Cargo heritors thereof. David thought the Frank Lloyd Wright chairs less uffish than
     Mackintosh
and so you see the history of Modernism inscribed in, Spenser might say, their furniture,
     "The Dead" 's
cubby pantry creaking overhead. That's another device, Name It Again, the choleric
     uncle choleric,
table mentioned page four receiving glass p. 9 as we hop from clue to clue, Guinness mynas
     lapping up report.
It's all around you. What's a mirror, a romantic thing? *Our* writers see the film like a
     window's
on it, criticize the frame, judicious inviteds kibitzing the game. Annalee smells cellar damp,
Lisa admires a point about the bourgeois French, even Mann, how they give themselves to
     observation
kind as a cycle of fashion, thing knowing itself only drawn toward, as if asking them
to open car trunks there are puppets (looking like Nijinsky), in yellow jerkins with red trim
clashing with baked enamel, onlooker, we lift like ventriloquist dummies or the banners in
religious processions, the kind I saw invade my square and painted with vigil light
cadmium, square dab. Perhaps the realists want it waving on poles, to be declared beautiful
     as Hobbes said
we're not damned for, a quantum admiration natural, so it's wrong in a way to present the
     pretty servant girl
as fact, her eyes perhaps pale as peridot. Too much of Realism seems to want
the dingy cuff for outline, as I recall my first live *Arsenic's* Jonathan's facial scar
was (I was curious to see) red lined both sides with black, the man on other days a
     churchgoer, I think an usher.
But all we really find revolting is that no one's jacket is lined in red, no counterjumper
hiding in fat wallet a flattened primrose, pimpernel, which if discovered would have
the police on him, the secrets they guard banal as a rote epithet. Stevenson is more than
     observation urging
the flashlight under the raincoat, that you hiding in murk bear light to a rendezvous.
It is like the word interrupt in French, ka-whump, that which we don't for Realists
with care, not going armed to the boxing match, the rules are game's, these men
will be shot at dawn, or tested.

Art and Industry

Adam Smith's opera singers and buffoons, though nonproductive workers, give pleasure to
drones, capitalists, landowners, perhaps useful to remember the distinction
between entertainment and art some theorists urge as absolute.
So the writer whom Pound argues cleanses language is though marginal
of some importance, productive in a way of a general well-being,
and alternate force to the rise and dominance of proletarian slang.
In such terms the Dismal Science attacks the arts, like a
bad debt. But add to this the Derridean analysis which sees
each reader of the *Cantos* as a little author . . . adding real labor to it.
Oeconomy will ask is this a battery or solitaire, "energy" one of those concepts
like "labor," "force," important as reciprocally defined. Imagine after all
this talk of "commodity" you want a real model (a little machine, Smith
said it was) for imaginative writing, *Ulysses* or Jekyll and Hyde, the dripping,
fly-buttoning post-Flaubert petty culture described as if described as if sung,
or the romantics' imbalance as part of the product, not object but
reproducible experience in which you are complicit but no more own than as
Marcel says you own your body. And Pieper has a point—the cant of work
infects discussion of genius, not all labor repetitive, predictable, the wild surmise
itself, years later, productive of something like wild surmise. Utterson rewarded the
authors of *Noctes Ambrosianae,* who entertained like Holmes's (more democratic)
Autocrat, but saved in order to command, later, more results of labor, the
cash of this imagined man (glorious narrator of *Jekyll*) not docketed for prodigality
but as we said time-bound. It was the class of advocates in France, appointed
honoraries, who by luck, ability and an invisible place in the culture, preserved the
    aristocracy.
If poems or novels are red robes they fall in the cracks, their matrices metaphors.
You don't extirpate "up," "down," or reward them. They are of that
class of beings which do not exhaust themselves in use, vampires and angels,
"forgiveness," the noose in Punch, contemporary sculpture's stone machines.

Transforming Machines

Brudniak kept a wee octopus in a jar with fluid he confessed is car—antifreeze, something
    of the sort—slung under a theodolite tripod remounted with complex small parts from
    adding machine or
something, and a hornlike flaring square tube aiming roughly at you at the end, a switch
I hadn't seen and wouldn't think to press with *a* still (forget what) on a small screen midway
    recessed
in the tube which moves, swivels—all really very touchable, pretty as old
equipment unfamiliar by accident you see in shops, surplusage, pawn.
To start with one is sceptical—here's this squid, cephalopod, guaranteed interest, simply
    added to a
pretty but very flat assemblage. Other things of his seem to incorporate, uneasily, organic
    matter.
Mostly you've big glass cases like what you put a quarter in and fish for dice,
the big rare few more of a heaviness—pure-rust refrigerator you can open, a
square hole through kiln brick or something to bright interior, window as if the light were
    being kept.

And then let into a wall heaviest door, glass porthole a face through (his, he says, so gold
you need be told), its eye receiving without wince a thin visible laser beam, red,
reflected off little dental mirrors, it seems, more delicate than bendable rugose gaspipe
protecting electric cords, presented as operative preserving device for sculptor.
This is buffoonery, like the guy in the Whitney who does giant Polaroid cameras and coffins
with mighty chromed posts and eyelets. Steve instead's an eye that looks appraising.
Easy to imagine stories told himself, little myths, about what mock-connections do, the
fun he has just not ours, as Manet got to look at Morisot hours, painting that balcony,
getting the greens just right.
It is, with metal and cement, *Watership Down* equivalent, pawky, fey, often a bit of insolence
not too concealed, hologramic eyes you see are (peering) eyes, bits you hold that as you
approach
other bits skroink or whonk.
Is this sculpture, then, or saving-and-presenting? Whom do we thank. The Jungians will ask
where Soul resides, tapping the fridge, tucking a passport covertly between mirror
and laser, wanting (I fear) to be part of it, as on midways one wants to be up there
demonstrating things to be done with liquid. The soul here (in these pieces) is solid,
is made of metal, so what happens, properly residence rather than plot, is like sculptures
thinking, dare we say, in some metallic italic, *dreaming themselves,* or is this a hoax
and these are us as usual dreaming our Coney Island everyday vending plots like what
you see
on television every day but brass, yeah, and chrome, duh marriage porthole screw, that any
machine you touch you're in a sense inside, your gold face eye rescattering directed light.

Leland's Paper Boat

Hickman, the brutality of address reserved for people not met, and editors contains for me
the acknowledgement
of a distance that might be made less. The wariness wears away mistakable for boy's
school heartiness . . .
come to by the poems, a line quoted by Robert Peters about a bird found in a forest, hence a
fan letter to Beyond Baroque, and a flashy *Bachy* back then *Great Slave Lake,* the
suite of. Given today "in my hand" as W. C. Williams would say a new tomato just picked,
pale yellow to red-orange darker than the old Crayola, minutes after reading about Lee
whom I wanted to please by writing something about his *Suite.*

The old lines look like Vachel Lindsay, boomlay-boom: *I can make it/all, yr frycook
cuss wingspan riveter teethsuck flat times flat/broke ball-peen clawhammer crosscut
bevel, level,/plane*
for what who told him might be James Joyce out of Thomas Wolfe, parental splutter
built in to the lines as if Perry Mason always saying *objection,* elevated like the host or
Europe
to pitchlike song that whole experience of just those years, the young man how he suffers,
Infant
of Prague regretting pain, dressed in those robes. You're given as in *Temblor* everything,
masses of mashed potatoes, the richest pork gravy and grandfather manfully ignoring
maggots in the fish.

*

Being buried or not buried with father is comic, those handfuls because it makes no sense, what we
come to, squat burial urns in Sir Thomas Browne decorated any boring Saxon way
the parts just put in not as he thought burned beforehand, well we don't come to it, this
is not us, body incarcerated in ceramic not where love is nor exudate, squeezed out. The body's haloed bodies
shifting in a chair to open letters are one by courtesy, we've left hundreds of bodies like kleenex or Anzio
the nails pounding in *Slave Lake Suite* as he hunches into a black wreck, writing, a body
is what is called, love calling *us* to things of this world, the academic poet says.

Every two years that wonderful voice on the phone. You pull string between tin cups never farther
than a shout would carry, red-orange cap in the street: a child has been.
You hear in imagination the noise it made—not quite the same as impact in the ear.
We'd letters from him about dinners with the Eshlemans. Lists of food.
His life for me begins with his poem in stiff green boards, to a letter from Charles on pale blue
stationery with his name, the canceled stamps a wreath some years in length.
Give honor to the name and nature housed therein, the voice so disruptive.

The answer to slow time is how the body matures, the eagle's wrinkle, owl's plumage white as butter
and it is certainly hard not to think of being crucified on it, liquidity of eye
no sign of anything until you see how close to gel. Young Keats breathed out his lungs
until he hadn't any, just hollows the autopsy found, innocent of bronchioles you'd think you'd need
to breathe through, the organism reverting to brute surface, unelaborated tongue, nose. I weep
as may be for closed systems and integuments breached, egg smaller than a pair of dice
on sill or pavement, ephemerida in heaps by lakes, the sound (Chris says) of paper yellowing.

Pardon the dissertation incomplete, on your words so percussive reading's like self-auscultation
or watching someone crash a bicycle. I once, told to ride a mo-ped, ran into a car fender
ending upside-down, wheels turning, under it. Palavered about the dent but found a finger
under it pushed it right out, from behind. It's your words (I want to say) I need and here
they are, shrill in capitals in your poem so full of pain it's like Villon, something medieval
but everything else too, churchbells, horses, those fish, relatives so alive in us we are a chorus
or sometimes the Romantic ship you see over and over, just sailing on with nobody left aboard.

A Shot at Narrative

To bend Ithuriel to Abdiel's pattern—if Atticus were he—were to bedizen in some subjunctive state
the rag monster, Green Man in his foliage, Nijinsky's personating of Petroushka, diamond doll
which's marble hall squares elongate, mailslot flap become Italian stage, the flies much lowered

if in this oblong region pink and blue flit hither like pirates in *Peter Pan* gone daft
yet callable to order by their thumper's rod, beadled into crass complacency, felt patch at
middle cheekbone discardable as blush or juvenile tan powdered to an eggshell to take light
each lash a jewel, mouth corners ruby sequins—the true ruby with a touch of blue for soul
no wine described as ever has achieved. The ingenue's a mayfly scarce hatched when
    swooped on by
the Grackle King, but lo, keepers dressed in olive green in rescuing deposit her in
    Arachne's bower.
The set's clear soda straws, backlit in blue. She feigns mascara terror, Tarantule creeps
in, one leg at a time, and thinks a praise of Balanchine to interstitial passages of Berlioz, the
mayfly's prayer consonant as undernote. She hides in a bucket. Her wings absorb milk. A pink
tint to the cyclorama means it's dawn, the bad dark Shivas scuttle off to corners
and Iris dressed in net dyed in a range from coral to leaf green whirls in like Isadora
or Duty in Wordsworth, all piety of Constable sky sketches, innocence imagined as
    transparency
ending the scene, but the curtain drops Buchanan tartan, healthiest of plaids, and an actor
dressed like Plato hobbles out, reading the middle third of *Laws* (Jowett) revised to Sitwell
    slang.
Poor Crito comes on wringing his hands and is ignored. The bias of the audience is for
    spectacle,
like *Turandot* in Dallas, pearlized Glynda bubble lowered to dragon's couching claw
the goddess issued from as if a subway, her virtue legendary as her transport, opera Tardis.
I regret the floor (washed pink by Degas) refinished by naked men on knees in Caillebotte,
the burlap wads soakable in balsamic oils and walnut to the eye though the stage is really dry
and gives off puffs of dust as catchers field ballerinas, plates likewise off Chinese juggler
    wands
strike on their rims, bounce offstage like *Big Allis* tires, the Hollow Dancers' gray
gauze costumes flat around the mouth like 3P-O, the middle scene in *Beauty*
and the Beast convened, reimagined, and our mayfly eaten. Well, she was ours by
    convention only, peg
to pull Stravinsky (all spangles and domino) on a plank over the pit, his running shoes
the rounded kind so he can *roll* onto tiptoe, climactic Rustica gone plangent whine
and rising scrim reveals the orchestra, sideways like draining opened sardines
the Bremen Players, an ape on a donkey's back supporting in one upraised hand like Liberty
the Azcan chicken, burnt-sienna rooster, the last word coming from its Stirner throat.
Iniquity decorates the cage, plated wire impure. Gods ask of plot not even direction,
but simply that an interval's distinguishable (so almost any plot runs in both directions).
Story is the goddess 'Istonax, who lives on Feather Island in the Scillies, feeding on sailors
and seeds about equally. The story goes that once she was a counter girl
who so wanted to be in a film that, when offered the role of sound effects, she chattered off
becoming by successive diminution a name for quondam power like a stock tip.

Of Gatherers

"Such nations are so miserably poor from mere want they are frequently reduced, or
think themselves reduced, to the necessity of abandoning their infants, old people,
and those afflicted with lingering diseases," first page of Adam Smith, and so
we find we do as one's come on by a storm, say in the Lake District where it'll feel
as if we're found out, is this me, good heavens that was grandfather. Disease corrodes eld
    and AIDS

anyone so the storm is like memorial services too plentiful like children's gravestones.
I'm told I don't want my poems plain, angle for huh. You could delay anything, "imagine
my surprise" as if blue gentians, whatever those were rendered expressionist as a cube
     envelope
in warm brown space, what a surprise to see a many-fleuret flower, phlox, lilac, made
almost a single substance, planar, given Onderdonk attempts at fieldsful memorized
by dabble schools. Their planes in blue stippled yellow, white to show the little inside
     colors we know are there
are a survey of the effect of bluebonnet in bulk when what is wanted (say) is countable
     Matisse goldfish,
compassable bathers. Tuck in a few gatherers with baskets, Victorian truants as
mock raffish as Arthur Rackham gypsies in the *Compleat Angler.* You could say beef is
     like that
in portraits any century made of abattoirs. In the meantime we all thought coastal tribes
     hard pressed,
up early with their dibbles. In fact it seems with everyone working, and work includes
     knowing
when which roots will come up, the genuine lore, that coming of age in such potlatch cultures
was more leisurely not that there were no clocks but that they ran more slowly, everyone
     working
a staggered system and the noble males who hunted, with elaborate dances, masked spirits
     and couvade
lucky to put in ten percent of the take, the women menstruating like dogs. It would be string
     games
or Graves's celtic finger-codes keeping it in the head, and children trying out the new
     tomatoes, yams
the mouths streaked with forbidden, sometimes fatal, juice. Fish bones and pelts piled up,
and here we are again, cloyed with apparatus of preliteracy, traps made of reeds,
designs you'd think easy to get back. It doesn't work that way, their pouches and shoulder
     sacks
are not pockets, the model holsters for dolls modeled on the quiver as if children came
     nocked.

Old Shapes Revisited

Cambridge ladies taste like turpentine. The old creative writing school, workshop courses
would "give" you besides the word give these exercises, write (Sylvia) a poem
about those sheep, making them archetypal, on nonarchival Big Chief pads you bring to class
reserved like holy plate for this, a coffee ring, well you could *print* that on a napkin
to make it more "imaginative," this year's Blue Star gallery invitation dripping consequents,
     slit
here, here, cut sections folded parallel, handful of leaves die-cut, and this *is* their imagination,
     that
as you unfold it falls apart. Isuzu fires a good ad agency because (perhaps) having been
     consulted
it comes to think it knows. Voting feels like making. Each of them writing a
word or two got us *Exquisite Corpse,* the critical act after the fact appreciative as the
     adjective
enshrined like the bottle shape the board went for. We're paying always for the means
to achieve design. Well maybe a door opens in its stomach isn't as gripping as

the dog in *Secret Agent* yapping at the door, thumbprint left by crumbling Egyptian flax.
What kind of bridge (Edison's carbonized thread) does inference leap across?
Some huddles of words suggest they have been chosen on a principle, the sow's ear with cello,
Chaplin's serried lights meant to be a train's windows perfectly adequate. Our instinct
creates wholes, care, selection, from forest or a heap of pebbles, makes urban experience
a poem about a bridge, the scarlet *I* you wonder where she got the thread for.
Wind goes through the dandelion, severs petals. Poets write poems on napkins, and
what if Rauschenberg, sketching out a thing, got interested in ballpoint spreading wet
　　　through fibers?
Subjects give us hints, shake loose a limb to shake with as if students let loose in the Baptist
parking lot photograph each other, take off their clothes to make piles of cloth, shoepolish
ink a means of escape, descriptions of the faery lands forlorn from holograms of casements,
　　　nah, not
voting or simpleminded reconstruction but Marcel, saying "What would happen if we did
　　　without
spatial metaphor here, at all?" to an empty lecture hall, the students in the streets with Sartre
persuading them their minds were interesting from what occurred inside. Rats in the street
　　　could be
rearranged with bits of brick to be Delacroix's *Spirit of Liberty,* the rats *standing for* bodies,
hence pure, conceptual, no longer rats. Imagination's up on the roof, waving its tail—at least
that period's hadn't decided how to handle gasoline (our posters tired Leger according to
　　　Print).
Blazier raids a whole issue of *U&LC* to make a collage called Plot because the word's
　　　incorporated,
wondering if he did a T-shirt run could they sue. Actually he said *would* they, a more
　　　interesting question
wired in parallel to the practical. Today we compared Barbie and the Little Mermaid
　　　anatomically,
the one's slip-on tail flukes horizontal as Moby-Dick's, her undulations consequently
　　　horizontal.
Imagination, far from being a wrinkle on a thing, can even be Raphael's boring trick
of making it like everyone else's, a bit better, the British garden spade imported rather than
the bronze frog handle on your garden faucet, whatever this might feel like through your
　　　flowered glove
or if the potholder instead of a fish were shaped like Husserl's mailbox.

State of the Art

From little mining towns to metropoli, controlled by refuse. The thread of your life jams,
to be cut like umbilicus, with the teeth. We see an atmosphere luminous, coming from hearth,
weird sisters in rags or naked sharing scissors and an eye. A lamb boils.
The scissors (medieval, two blades on a spring) hung from coarse thread turns North.
Pits on the wall could be constellations. It's the horror story of English poetry, Roethke's
legs out from under the potting bench while he's enchanted by fleshy hairy root systems,
writes them up, shuddering Swift the patient etherized. We're wounded by omissions, each
　　　slug
a Tyger. A glass offered you is perspiration, or the bottom thick as a coke bottle
whips out a monocle. The instant of recognition is foreign, some lad
from another century sweeping horse dung. Almost any remark occurs in the context
　　　poverty.

Feel the root fibers and filaments, so like an excretory protection system, shaved belly of
one's neutered cat going back to fleece, primordial tum. Vampire bears on night hunts
suck bats to leather gargoyles, strapped tea strainers over eye sockets. Corpses dug up
are found compromisingly posed. Postcards inform friends you intended Yugoslavia. In
　　verse you can
say Dubrovnik. A scribbled grant could be a napkin, glue your old passport to canvas.
Small bottles of Perrier inverted bleed into feet, are glasses.
Animals stuffed with messages or cookies degrade in shops. The sound of eating is the
　　sound of reading.
Dogs, sewed up in lamb skins, whisper repent, or wittily property is use. They run the farm,
　　defer to pigs.
No one, absolutely no one, cares what you do.

A Map of Misreading

Frank Harris, who sometimes signed himself *Sirrah Knarf,* to evade the US censors, won
　　me by remarking
he'd never seen the British habit of preferring Shelley to Keats, citing all the right texts.
　　Georg Brandes,
for instance, quotes whole stanzas of "West Wind" and "The Cloud," unaware that
　　syllables next to each other
even in one inscribed *Cor cordis,* approved not really an atheist by Trelawny (who says it was
to confound the righteous) are not terribly interesting . . . perhaps his peacock screech in
　　those *e*'s
makes his sound reedy as his readers's, thin the way *Testament of Beauty* is thin, almost
　　saying to you
you've not got the trick of reading me quite yet. Clio was just reading Edmund Wilson on
　　detective stories,
things his friends made him read, observing he (reducing them to puzzles) skims what isn't,
　　leaving a
pretty trick revealed, the corpse in belfry succumbed to sound, nothing aficionados didn't
　　figure by page four.
The hostile reader aims his hobbyhorse and rocks, as Keats made fun of Pope though
　　they'd have much
to talk about, tricks and so on, how I got over that consonantal cluster, symposia on
　　slowing down a line, ways to
slow one down. Then there were witches, the elbows of which extend skin-piercing bark,
　　"Elyda, your
time has come, Elyda!" It isn't always critics, though Philip Herrera (*Time,* 1973) by
　　imitating Lovecraft's mannerisms
thinks to be funny by showing how easy it is, review by pastiche, as Sin perhaps chivvies
　　Satan in *Paradise Lost*
the way the scholar Knight of Mirrors chaffs Quixote, "Friend, you sound thus" and we're
　　to go right in the head,
when quoting us in print is quite enough. Today in BookStop's periodical shelf *Exquisite
　　Corpse* stuck up like a
pulp crest has my poem tucked in, appearance already quotation acknowledging context.
　　The piece you write enlarges
for that issue your periphery. The orange juice goes bad in the fridge. The dog's forelegs are
　　shorter.

Weedy children of people who hounded Shelley out of Oxford memorize *Alastor,* the
   references in Quiller-Couch or Bradley's
Oxford Lectures increasingly respectful. A study of Young Nietzsche says he learned to be
   misunderstood's
a sign you're good and having learned the knack Aufhebunged himself, Freud's rows
   (under glass and not) of brass
gods and goddies homage to Max Müller, herrs for whom anything arcane (neither Greek
   nor Christian) properly
peopled a study, plaque not suggestive of the Parthenon. For us Puvis in aquatint, cut out
   from a journal
'd announce allegiance, like a holy card in a missal when *holy card* meant *poker chip,* the
   counter
paid for by acquiescing to a formality. In the basements of the Vatican documents proving
   violation of nuns
by confessors, by Monk Lewis, Frank Harris, yellow on shelves inaccessible to the laity,
   the authors, hah,
snuffed out like firstborn Egyptians, authors whose last names end *is* preserved endlessly,
   Rabelais, Novalis.

To the Virgins

I'm tempted to say, to make much of me. Actually experience in the relatively young yields
   charm
and poise, I think, what Chevalier thanked Heaven for in little "girls," the British novel
about the man blackmailed for having it with a kid sane enough in its sound, though a thriller.
Nabokov may by confronting early that kind of appeal stave off a lack, and it is sometimes
possible to surprise complicity in a gaze, that could unsettle you for days. One needs (some
wisdom says) to be on guard if girls and boys are only by convention nonsexual. Carroll
posing Liddell for his camera with the wonderful lens, hiking up a skirt here and there
could lecture on the darkroom compromise developed from surmise, an odd wish rejoicing
   in excess
of life staring at you roundeyed from the rectangle dish. Glass sensitized, or bedsheet as in
   Tafi's
cyanoprints from negatives exposed like laundry on a bush, dark blues for blacks, cut by
   her out and sewn
to quilts disconcert, these patterned house-construction beams and pop in silhouette, our
   Mr. Brown
wry in his director's chair ends up a pillow there, tuck in-able, the small of back eased by
   one's front.
It's everywhere, removing a book from library shelf, digit on spine, the gap. You make
us choose over and over innocence, Lowell's poems to booze the blessing of one activity
by quite another, temptation the red herring, even Francesca's device of flirting with
   flirtation too abstract
for what, again, is luscious in the hole in dirt left when you flip over the pebble, in (say)
the rust deposited selectively on a drying facecloth drawn to extremities, promise in
Brooke Shields's eyebrows of pigment in the vein, of anything with eyes photographed,
what the doll's lids close so they won't see, glass irises rolling with that motion down and in.

110

Index

DALKEY ARCHIVE PAPERBACKS

FICTION: AMERICAN

BARNES, DJUNA. *Ladies Almanack*	9.95
BARNES, DJUNA. *Ryder*	9.95
COOVER, ROBERT. *A Night at the Movies*	9.95
CRAWFORD, STANLEY. *Some Instructions to My Wife*	7.95
DOWELL, COLEMAN. *Too Much Flesh and Jabez*	8.00
DUCORNET, RIKKI. *The Fountains of Neptune*	10.95
GASS, WILLIAM H. *Willie Masters' Lonesome Wife*	9.95
MARKSON, DAVID. *Springer's Progress*	9.95
MARKSON, DAVID. *Wittgenstein's Mistress*	9.95
McELROY, JOSEPH. *Women and Men*	15.95
SEESE, JUNE AKERS. *Is This What Other Women Feel Too?*	9.95
SEESE, JUNE AKERS. *What Waiting Really Means*	7.95
SORRENTINO, GILBERT. *Aberration of Starlight*	9.95
SORRENTINO, GILBERT. *Imaginative Qualities of Actual Things*	9.95
SORRENTINO, GILBERT. *Splendide-Hôtel*	5.95
SORRENTINO, GILBERT. *Steelwork*	9.95
SORRENTINO, GILBERT. *Under the Shadow*	9.95
STEPHENS, MICHAEL. *Season at Coole*	7.95
WOOLF, DOUGLAS. *Wall to Wall*	7.95
YOUNG, MARGUERITE. *Miss MacIntosh, My Darling*	2-vol. set, 30.00
ZUKOFSKY, LOUIS. *Collected Fiction*	9.95

FICTION: BRITISH

CHARTERIS, HUGO. *The Tide Is Right*	9.95
FIRBANK, RONALD. *Complete Short Stories*	9.95
MOSLEY, NICHOLAS. *Accident*	9.95
MOSLEY, NICHOLAS. *Impossible Object*	9.95
MOSLEY, NICHOLAS. *Judith*	10.95

FICTION: FRENCH

ERNAUX, ANNIE. *Cleaned Out*	9.95
GRAINVILLE, PATRICK. *The Cave of Heaven*	10.95
NAVARRE, YVES. *Our Share of Time*	9.95
QUENEAU, RAYMOND. *The Last Days*	9.95
QUENEAU, RAYMOND. *Pierrot Mon Ami*	7.95
ROUBAUD, JACQUES. *The Great Fire of London*	12.95
SIMON, CLAUDE. *The Invitation*	9.95

DALKEY ARCHIVE PAPERBACKS

FICTION: IRISH

Cusack, Ralph. *Cadenza*	7.95
MacLochlainn, Alf. *Out of Focus*	5.95
O'Brien, Flann. *The Dalkey Archive*	9.95

FICTION: LATIN AMERICAN

Valenzuela, Luisa. *He Who Searches*	8.00

FICTION: SPANISH

Tusquets, Esther. *Stranded*	9.95

POETRY

Alfau, Felipe. *Sentimental Songs (La poesía cursi)*	9.95
Ansen, Alan. *Contact Highs: Selected Poems 1957-1987*	11.95
Burns, Gerald. *Shorter Poems*	9.95
Fairbanks, Lauren. *Muzzle Thyself*	9.95
Theroux, Alexander. *The Lollipop Trollops*	10.95

NONFICTION

Gazarian Gautier, Marie-Lise. *Interviews with Latin American Writers*	14.95
Gazarian Gautier, Marie-Lise. *Interviews with Spanish Writers*	14.95
Mathews, Harry. *20 Lines a Day*	8.95
Roudiez, Leon S. *French Fiction Revisited*	14.95
Shklovsky, Viktor. *Theory of Prose*	14.95

For a complete catalog of our titles, or to order any of these books, write to Dalkey Archive Press, Fairchild Hall/ISU, Normal, IL 61761. One book, 10% off; two books or more, 20% off; add $3.00 postage and handling. Phone orders: (309) 438-7555.